6th edition

W0284165

FOCUS on success

ALLGEMEINE AUSGABE

Lösungsbeileger für Workbook mit Skills Training

von
James Abram
Michael Benford
Steve Williams

unter Mitarbeit der Verlagsredaktion

Cornelsen

1 Holidays and tourism

WORKING WITH WORDS

1 ACTIVITIES AND HOLIDAYS

A/B

	Activities		Type of holiday
1	*stay* at home	*relax* on your balcony	*staycation*
2	*go* canyoning	*do* something exciting	*activity* holiday
3	*sleep* in a tent	not *stay* in hotels	*camping* holiday
4	*see* new sights	*have* a wonderful time	*sightseeing* holiday
5	*lie* in the sun	*do* nothing	*beach* holiday
6	*hitchhike* around Europe	*travel* by train	*backpacking* holiday

2 SAFARI TOUR

2 Destination/ National Park
3 (Tour) Guides
4 Transport(ation)
5 Accommodation
6 Washing facilities
7 Attractions
8 Meals and refreshments/drinks
9 Power points
10 Money
11 Visa requirements
12 Vaccinations
13 Travel insurance

GRAMMAR

1 WORD ORDER

individuelle Lösungen

2 PERSONAL PRONOUNS AND POSSESSIVE ADJECTIVES

1 **A** Hi, Becky. Hi, Simon. Have **you** got a portable charger? I can't find **my** charger anywhere. Maybe **I** lost **it** somewhere.
B Hi, Lauren. Sure, **you** can borrow **our** charger. **We** aren't using it right now.

2 **A** Kip took **me** to see a family of lions yesterday. **He** said **they** were really difficult to find.
B I'd love to have **his** job. **He** spends all **his** time with wild animals.

3 **A** I hate this campsite! **Its** washing facilities aren't as clean as the others. I don't like using **them** at all.
B What does Deanna say? I think **we** should all complain to **her** about **them**.

4 **A** Hi, Lauren. Could **you** take a photo of the two of **us**? We want to send **it** to our grandchildren. So **they** can see what **their** grandparents are doing on safari.

3 SIMPLE PRESENT *VS* PRESENT PROGRESSIVE

1 don't like; **2** think, **3** stay; **4** find; **5** love; **6** come, **7** say; **8** 'm taking; **9** 'm sitting; **10** am watching; **11** are enjoying; **12** is shining; **13** are standing; **14** is; **15** decide; **16** is wearing; **17** isn't; **18** are still pouring; **19** have to

BUILDING SKILLS

PREPARING TO READ

A
b

B
individuelle Lösungen

C
paragraph 1: a / paragraph 2: d / paragraph 3: b / not used: c

D
1 two-thirds
2 the rise of influencers
3 to make family and friends jealous / envy them
4 men: 20%; women 10%

2 Adventure sports

WORKING WITH WORDS

1 WORD FIELD: SPORTS

A

S	X	T	R	A	**K**	**T**	M	N	P	**G**	Q	W	X	Y
C	P	O	I	**C**	J	**E**	H	G	**N**	**O**	R	X	C	E
I	Q	W	**A**	E	R	**N**	T	**I**	Z	**L**	U	I	P	O
T	**D**	**R**	S	D	F	**N**	**R**	G	H	**F**	J	K	L	V
E	**T**	**N**	Y	**P**	X	**I**	**C**	**E**	**H**	**O**	**C**	**K**	**E**	**Y**
L	C	V	**O**	B	**O**	**S**	N	M	Q	W	E	**R**	T	Z
H	U	I	P	**M**	**C**	**O**	**S**	**W**	**I**	**M**	**M**	**I**	**N**	**G**
T	**P**	A	S	**O**	**A**	D	**L**	F	G	**T**	H	**N**	K	**N**
A	Q	**I**	**U**	W	E	**I**	R	T	**R**	Z	U	**K**	A	**I**
S	D	**R**	**T**	F	G	H	**D**	**U**	J	K	Y	X	C	**X**
V	**S**	B	N	**C**	**F**	**O**	**O**	**T**	**B**	**A**	**L**	**L**	M	**O**
E	M	Y	C	V	**H**	**C**	**L**	**L**	**A**	**B**	**E**	**S**	**A**	**B**

ATHLETICS TRACK; ICE HOCKEY RINK; TENNIS COURSE; GOLF COURSE; SWIMMING POOL; BASEBALL DIAMOND; BOXING RING; FOOTBALL PITCH

B

Tennis: racket, ball, shoes, shirt, shorts, ...
Swimming: trunks, costume, goggles, ...
Golf: ball, clubs, tee, ...
Baseball: bat, glove, mouthguard, ...
Athletics: shirt, shoes, shorts, ...
Football: ball, shirt, shoes, shorts, ...
Ice-hockey: helmet, ice skates, stick, mouthguard, ...
Boxing: gloves, mouthguard, shorts, shoes, ...

2 WORDS THAT ARE EASILY CONFUSED

1 plays, trains
2 does, go
3 had, fell, hit
4 break
5 practising, teaching
6 performing, makes
7 gets, survive, pay

GRAMMAR

1 SIMPLE PAST

1 made; **2** was; **3** drove; **4** went; **5** didn't jump; **6** had; **7** took; **8** threw; **9** knew; **10** opened; **11** taught

2 PRESENT PERFECT WITH *SINCE* OR *FOR*

1 has taught – for
2 has done – since
3 has been – since
4 has lived – since
5 haven't jumped – for
6 have had – for

3 SIMPLE PAST *VS* PRESENT PERFECT

1 answered; **2** had got; **3** have been; **4** for; **5** have never seen; **6** said; **7** survived; **8** had fallen; **9** caught; **10** stopped; **11** meant; **12** laughed; **13** was / has been; **14** have ever taken part; **15** commented; **17** since; **18** has become

BUILDING SKILLS

DEALING WITH UNKNOWN WORDS

	Original word	Prefix	Suffix	New word form	Meaning
coexistence	*exist (v)*	*co-*	*-ence*	*n*	*Zusammenleben*
disagreement	*agree (v)*	*dis-*	*-ment*	*n*	*Meinungsverschiedenheit*
resurface	*surface (v/n)*	*re-*	—	*v*	*wiederauftauchen*
antisocial	*social (adj)*	*anti-*	—	*adj*	*unsozial, asozial*
irresponsible	*responsible (adj)*	*ir-*	—	*adj*	*unverantwortlich*
environmental	*environment (n)*	—	*-al*	*adj*	*Umwelt-*
organization	*organize (v)*	—	*-ation*	*n*	*Organisation*
transformation	*transform (v)*	*trans-*	*-ation*	*n*	*Umwandlung*
damaging	*damage (v)*	—	*-ing*	*adj*	*schädlich*
dangerous	*danger (n)*	—	*-ous*	*adj*	*gefährlich*
recovery	*cover (v)*	*re-*	*-y*	*n*	*Bergung*
internationally	*nation (n)*	*inter-*	*-ally*	*adv*	*international*
disagree	*agree (v)*	*dis-*	—	*v*	*widersprechen*
statistically	*statistic (n)*	—	*-ally*	*adv*	*statistisch*
impossible	*possible (adj)*	*im-*	—	*adj*	*unmöglich*
unlikely	*likely (adj)*	*un-*	—	*adj*	*unwahrscheinlich*
co-operation	*operate (v)*	*co-*	*-ation*	*n*	*Zusammenarbeit*

3 My image, my style

WORKING WITH WORDS

1 BODY IMAGE: VERBS

1 encourages; **2** inspired; **3** acknowledge; **4** relate; **5** shamed; **6** celebrate; **7** glamorizing; **8** promoting

2 BODY IMAGE: COLLOCATIONS

1 role model; **2** sense of humour; **3** body positivity; **4** cosmetic surgery; **5** plus-sized; **6** self-conscious; **7** low self-esteem; **8** airbrushed images; **9** tattoo artist

3 WORD FORMATION

Verb	Noun (person / thing)	Noun (abstract)
to employ	*employer / employee*	*employment*
to labour	*labourer*	labour
to manufacture	*manufacturer*	*manufacturing*
to consume	*consumer*	consumption / consumerism
to manage	*manager*	management
to contribute	*contributor*	*contribution*

GRAMMAR

1 SOME, ANY, MUCH, MANY, A LOT OF

1 Rishi has got **some** tattoos but he hasn't got **any** piercings.
2 How **many** tattoos has he got altogether?
3 Is there **anywhere** on his body that isn't covered in tattoos?
4 He doesn't have **a lot of** tattoos on his chest, but there are **a lot** on his arms.
5 How **much** money has he spent on tattoos? – **A lot**!
6 Rishi has **some** plans for new tattoos. He always has **a lot of** good ideas.

2 FEW, LITTLE, LOT(S), MUCH

1 a lot of / lots of
2 little
3 A few – a lot of / lots of
4 a little – much
5 few
6 much – few

3 UNCOUNTABLE NOUNS

1 was; **2** garbage; **3** rubbish is; **4** advice; **5** information; **6** behaviour; **7** is; **8** is; **9** research shows; **10** damage; **11** damage; **12** waste

BUILDING SKILLS

READING FOR GIST

A
1 mass-produced, cheap fashion items
2 to be out of date, no longer fashionable
3 app/website where people can swap items of clothing
4 to question or threaten sth
5 society that produces a lot of waste

B
1e, 2a, 3b, 4c
Heading not used: d

C
b

4 Stress and pressure

WORKING WITH WORDS

1 WORDFIELD: SUNEUNG

1 pressure; **2** School leavers; **3** prestigious; **4** prospects; **5** income; **6** degree; **7** burden; **8** extracurricular; **9** isolation; **10** well-being; **11** revision; **12** tutors; **13** ranking

2 WORD FORMATION

Verb	Noun	Verb	Noun
to abuse	*abuse*	to judge	*judgement*
to cure	*cure*	to press	*pressure*
to enforce	*enforcement*	to recover	*recovery*
to guide	*guidance*	to surrender	*surrender*
to influence	*influence*	to treat	*treatment*

3 PHRASAL VERBS

1e, 2h, 3a, 4f, 5b, 6d, 7c, 8g

GRAMMAR

1 ADJECTIVES AND ADVERBS

1 important, seriously
2 organized, diligently
3 Usually, private, normally
4 well, prestigious, tough
5 hard, anxious
6 depressed, scared

2 COMPARING ADJECTIVES AND ADVERBS

1 Haru works **harder than** Seok, but **not as hard as** Yuri. Jin works **the hardest** of them all.
2 Haru's score was **lower than** than Seok's but **not as low as** Jin's. Yuri had **the lowest** score of them all.
3 Jin's hogwan is **not as cheap as** Seok's but it is **cheaper** than Haru's. Yuri's hogwan is **the cheapest.**
4 Yuri's hogwan has **the highest** exam pass rate, as it is **higher** than Jin's. The exam pass rate for Haru's hogwan is **as high as** Jin's but it is **not as high as** Yuri's.
5 Seok explains things to his friends just **as well as** Jin, but Haru explains things even **better than** Seok. Yuri explains things **the best** of them all.
6 The conditions in Seok's hogwan are **worse than** than in Jin's, but **not as bad as** in Haru's. The conditions in Yuri's hogwan are **the worst** of them all.
7 Jin reads **more thoroughly than** Yuri, but **not as thoroughly as** Seok does. Haru reads **the most thoroughly** of them all.

BUILDING SKILLS

ANALYSING STATISTICS

A
A pie chart; **B** bar chart; **C** line graph

B
1 B, **2** C, **3** A, **4** A, **5** B, **6** C, **7** B, C, **8** A

C
1 The pie chart shows the different type of drug-related crimes as a percentage of the total for the month of January.
2 The bar chart shows the total drug-related crimes in thousands for the months of January to June.
3 This line graph shows the amount of drug sales in millions of euros for the years 2020 to 2020.

D
individuelle Lösungen

MAIN COURSE

5 My working life

WORKING WITH WORDS

1 COLLOCATIONS WITH 'JOB'

to *lose*	your	job	*gekündigt werden*
to *apply for*	a		*sich bewerben*
to *have*	a *part-time*		*Teilzeit arbeiten*
to *offer* sb	a		*einen Job anbieten*
to *quit*	your		*kündigen*
to *create*		jobs	*Arbeitsplätze schaffen*

2 NOUN COLLOCATIONS

1 Job **satisfaction** is one of the main requirements for young people when deciding on a career. As they are more likely to change jobs than their parents, job **security** is not considered so important.
2 Working **conditions** are also important, including working hours and **shift** work.
3 For people who are not self-employed, health **insurance,** sick **pay,** pension **contributions** and social **security** are all taken for granted in Germany.
4 For those people working freelance or in the gig economy, these benefits are not included, along with paid **leave** or an annual **holiday.**
5 Some of the most popular job **benefits** are a subsidized **canteen** and a company **car.**
6 Career or promotion **prospects** also play an important role.

3 WORD FORMATION

1 expansion, **2** exploitation, **3** independent, **4** flexible, **5** protection, **6** liable, **7** abundant, **8** competition, **9** insecurity

GRAMMAR

1 THE FUTURE: SIMPLE PRESENT AND PRESENT PROGRESSIVE

A **Are you coming** to my party tomorrow evening?
B I hope so. But tomorrow **is** my first day at my internship with Smith Partners.
A They're in London, aren't they? How **are you getting** there tomorrow morning?

B My Mum **is taking** me to the station to make sure I get the train on time. It **leaves** at 7.15.
A Cool! So will you make it to my party?
B My train **arrives** at 6.45 and Dad **is picking** me up from the station.

2 THE FUTURE: *WILL*-FUTURE AND *GOING TO*-FUTURE

1 'm/am going to start; **2** 'm/am going to leave; **3** will be; **4** 'll/will give; **5** is going to pay; **6** 'll/will be; **7** 'm/am not going to work; **8** 'll/will still have; **9** 'm/am going to be; **10** Will you have

3 THE FUTURE: MIXED TENSES

A
1 is starting; **2** will give; **3** 's/is going to deliver; **4** start, **5** don't/won't finish; **6** is going to quit; **7** 's/is starting; **8** begins; **9** finishes; **10** will give

B
individuelle Lösungen

SKILLS: READING

1 UNDERSTANDING THE TEXT

A
c

B
1 less than £4 an hour
2 1,189 microworkers
3 95%
4 roughly 30%
5 India, Kenya, Venezuela, (UK)

2 READING FOR DETAIL

A
1
- identifying and captioning images
- entering data / data entry
- clicking on ads

2
- people forced to work from home during pandemic
- low wages in UK / cost of living crisis

3
- not classified as employees (under employment law)
- (at least half an hour) unpaid activities per hour of paid work

B
paragraph 7: b, c
paragraph 8: a, f

C
- no relationship with the people they work for
- difficult to contact platforms if there are technical problems
- work can be rejected (and not paid)
- not suitable as a main source of income

SKILLS: WRITING

1 UNDERSTANDING THE TASK

A
b

B
d

2 COLLECTING IDEAS

A
Lösungsvorschlag:
- flexible working hours > *more time for family*
- salary/paycheck > *may be necessary to take a pay cut*
- burnout > *danger of burnout from working too many hours*
- career/promotion prospects > *not so important for many young people*
- employers > *often reluctant; only see people wanting to work less hours*
- white-collar workers > *mainly better paid workers who can demand flexible hours; not available to people from other sectors*
- remote working > *work connected to phone, not place of work*
- (own ideas) *gender inequality > housework and childcare still mainly responsibility of female workers*

3 STRUCTURING YOUR IDEAS

A
Lösungsvorschlag:
possible arguments for:
- burnout: danger of burnout from working too many hours
- flexible working hours: more time for family
- remote working: work connected to phone, not place of work

possible arguments against:
- employers: often reluctant; only see people wanting to work less hours
- white-collar workers: mainly better paid workers who can demand flexible hours; not available to people from other sectors
- gender inequality: housework and childcare still mainly responsibility of female workers

B
individuelle Lösungen

4 INTRODUCING THE DISCUSSION

Lösungsvorschlag:

refer to the topic/question/statement of the essay:	a, b, c, d
explain what the essay is going to do:	a, b, c, d
use impersonal, neutral language:	c
be short and concise:	a, b, c

c is the best option as it combines all the requirements.

5 WRITING THE DISCUSSION

individuelle Lösungen (vgl. 2–4)

6 Connected worlds

WORKING WITH WORDS

1 COLLOCATIONS AND COMPOUNDS

appeal to someone's conscience; echo chamber; engage with someone's views; free of charge; get access to; go viral; mobile device; multi-tasking; on the go; open-minded; reading preferences; reinforce someone's views

2 SOCIAL MEDIA ADJECTIVES

A

S	P	R	O	M	A	N	T	I	C	E
A	R	T	I	F	I	C	I	A	L	X
S	E	S	N	A	R	K	Y	U	A	U
H	T	F	H	O	N	E	S	T	U	B
I	E	A	S	O	C	A	L	H	G	E
N	N	K	U	F	L	A	S	E	H	R
G	T	E	G	U	S	H	I	N	G	A
A	I	N	T	E	R	E	S	T	R	N
H	O	S	T	I	L	E	N	I	E	T
A	U	W	H	I	M	S	I	C	A	L
T	S	I	N	C	E	R	E	I	N	G

1 sincere; **2** exuberant; **3** snarky; **4** authentic; **5** honest; **6** hostile; **7** pretentious; **8** artificial; **9** romantic; **10** whimsical; **11** gushing; **12** fake

3 CORRECT WORD

2 brands, clients
3 content, schedule
4 develop, filter
5 credibility, integrity
6 contain, hold
7 advertisements, consumers
8 following, sponsoring
9 endorse, sponsor

GRAMMAR

1 THE PASSIVE: SPOTTING AND CORRECTING ERRORS

1 In recent decades, our news has **been** changed completely by new technology.
2 Live news **was** produced by broadcasting corporations.
3 Nowadays, articles, videos and podcasts are often **published** by the same organization on the same website.
4 The distinction between fact and opinion is being **lost** with the change to an informal and user-friendly presentation style.
5 The news has **been** made 'sexier' to grab our attention.
6 Clickbait is often **used** to arouse our curiosity.
7 Juicy gossip **is** promised by headlines which then aren't discussed in the actual story.
8 Fake news **is** sometimes reported even by respected news sources.

2 THE PASSIVE: COMPLETING SENTENCES

2 is read; **3** is chosen; **4** was stopped; **5** was shared; **6** will be used; **7** be exposed; **8** has not been verified; **9** was transformed; **10** will be introduced; **11** will be improved; **12** will be made

SKILLS: LISTENING

1 PREPARING TO LISTEN: UNDERSTANDING THE GIST

a3, **b**5, **c**6, **d**4, **e**1, f2

2 MULTIPLE MATCHING

1d, **2**f, **3**a, **4**c   Headings not used: b, e

3 PREPARING TO LISTEN

1 Advertisements follow users who show interest in the product but *do not buy it.*
2 Cookies pass on our information to *other websites we visit.*
3 Political groups may want to *change how we vote.*
4 To avoid being tracked you *have to change* your online behaviour.

4 QUESTIONS ON THE TEXT

1 They follow us around because the advertisers pay to use many different websites.
2 Advertisers concentrate on those people who are most likely to buy the product.
3 We give advertisers data through our browsing behaviour, by using free online apps, and through our social media use.
4 They can find ways to change our voting behav-iour
5 It might become less democratic in the future.
6 We can change our browser settings, avoid using popular search engines, browse anonymously and stop using social media.
7 The alternative is to accept that our data will be used.

SKILLS: MEDIATION

1 DIE AUFGABE ANALYSIEREN

Analyse der Mediationsaufgabe:
- Ursprungstext: Bursting the bubble
- Adressat: *Internetfreund*
- Medium/Textsorte: *E-Mail*
- Zweck: *Überzeugen, Social Media nicht aufzugeben*
- Sprachebene: *informell*

2 DEN INHALT ANALYSIEREN

A

A 5,6
B 8
C 9
D 10
E 11

B 1,2,3,4

C

a wenige, vertraute Quellen: immer dieselbe Zeitung, Nachrichtensendung; kaum Vergleiche wiedersprüchlicher Quellen; kaum Austausch mit Andersdenkenden

b Nachrichten aus diversen, nicht gewählten Quellen; kaum möglich, wenigen vertrauten Quellen treu zu bleiben; größere Informationsmengen; Möglichkeiten zum Austausch mit Leuten in vielen Ländern

c unterschiedliche Sichtweisen ausloten und Möglichkeiten für eine respektvolle Diskussion mit Andersgesinnten schaffen

3 VERFASSEN DER MEDIATION

Erwartungshorizont:
- passende informelle Anrede
- Vorstellung des Themas/Problems
- Darstellung, wie Menschen offline Informationen beschaffen (vgl. Abs. 5, 6, 10), z. B. wenige, vertraute Quellen: immer dieselbe Zeitung, Nachrichtensendung; kaum Vergleiche wiedersprüchlicher Quellen; kaum Austausch mit Andersdenkenden
- Darstellung, wie Menschen online Informationen beschaffen (vgl. Abs. 8, 9, 10), z. B. Nachrichten aus diversen, nicht gewählten Quellen; kaum möglich, wenigen vertrauten Quellen treu zu bleiben; größere Informationsmengen; Möglichkeiten zum Austausch mit Menschen in vielen Ländern
- Aufforderung, eine aufgeschlossene Weltanschauung bewusst zu pflegen, z. B. durch das Ausloten unterschiedlicher Sichtweisen und indem man Möglichkeiten für eine respektvolle Diskussion mit Andersgesinnten schafft
- passende Schlussformel

SKILLS: ANALYSING A CARTOON

1 ANALYSING THE TASK

a, b, c

2 DESCRIBING THE CARTOON

A

It depicts a busy café with individuals/friends sitting together.

B

Three young people are sitting at a table. One is texting and speaking, one is writing in a book and one is using a laptop. They have trendy hair and clothes. They look as if they have money. Two of the people have indifferent facial expressions, the third looks happy.

C

On the table there is a computer and a notebook, which are being used by two of the people. The third person is looking at his phone. Around them are backpacks. These aren't the usual objects you might see when three people meet. It looks as if the three are working and getting ideas. They might be freelancers, influencers, creative types.

D

There is a caption. One of the men says that he wants to achieve success and see it disappear.

3 ANALYSING THE CARTOON

A

This cartoon examines the role of social media in achieving success / how social media has changed our view of success.

B

The cartoonist makes fun of the idea that one can achieve success that disappears immediately.

C

The cartoon's message is that success or fame through social media is very short-term.

4 GIVING YOUR OPINION

A

Lösungsbeispiele:

I think that the cartoonist is using a lazy stereotype about young people on social media and does not really understand how social media influencing works.

I think that the cartoonist gives an accurate impression of the fleeting nature of social media.

B

Lösungsbeispiele:

The cartoon does not appeal to me personally, as it is too far removed from my experience.

I like the cartoon, because the people look as though they think they are important, but they aren't.

5 WRITING THE TEXT

Erwartungshorizont:

Description: café, three trendy young people using communication devices, caption about looking for influence/success (through social media)

Meaning: success or influence through social media = easy but short-lived / worthless

Opinion: lazy stereotype, inaccurate; or: humorous view of people who take themselves too seriously

7 Diversity in society

WORKING WITH WORDS

1 IDIOMATIC VERB PHRASES

1 Hey! You'**re freaking me out,** man! Do I need to **spell it out** to you! Go away!
2 My grandad **is getting on** a bit now. He's 87 and sometimes he can't **cope with** the everyday tasks in his life.
3 A: The pressure from my family **has been adding up** ever since I **came out** to them that I am gay. They still can't accept it and want me to keep quiet about it.
B: Hey, just **stand up to** them for once and tell them **to get real!** It's none of their business.
4 You ready to play, girl? I'm going to **kick your ass**! Let's get started!

2 WORD FAMILIES

Verb	Adjective	Noun (abstract)
to complicate	*complicated*	*complication*
to confuse	*confusing*	*confusion*
to forgive	*(un)forgiving*	*forgiveness*
to apologize	*apologetic*	*apology*

3 WORD BUILDING

2 disabilities; **3** acceptance; **4** participation; **5** integration; **6** challenging; **7** investment; **8** fundraising; **9** visibility; **10** socialize; **11** loneliness; **12** reputation; **13** impairments

GRAMMAR

1 SIMPLE PAST AND PAST PROGRESSIVE

1 was waiting, bumped
2 hit, was doing
3 was waiting, asked
4 started, told
5 asked, were swimming
6 were watching, was arguing

2 MODAL VERBS

1 Can/May/Might; **2** You should / ought to / must; **3** may/might; **4** can; **5** can; **6** mustn't; **7** needn't; **8** must / have to; **9** should / ought to; **10** can; **11** could/might

3 RELATIVE CLAUSES

1	which/that	5	who/that	9	(which/that)
2	(which/that)	6	whose	10	who
3	who/that	7	which/that	11	(that)
4	(which/that)	8	where		

SKILLS: READING

1 UNDERSTANDING THE TEXT

b

2 MULTIPLE CHOICE

A
a paragraphs 3 & 4
b paragraphs 5 & 6
c paragraphs 1 & 2

2B
1c, **2**a, **3**d

3 MULTIPLE MATCHING

A
a paragraph 9
b paragraph 2
c paragraph 8
d paragraph 6
e paragraph 7

3B
1c, **2**b, **3**e, **4**d, **5**a

SKILLS: WRITING

1 UNDERSTANDING THE TASK

b

2 COLLECTING ARGUMENTS

A/B

Arguments against accessibility	Arguments for accessibility
a) disability is a fact of life; can't be changed	b) everybody should have the same chances/ opportunities (principle of equality)
f) some physical barriers can't be changed easily, e.g. old buildings, histor-ic towns	e) some cities/countries have done a lot to re-move physical barriers

Arguments against accessibility	Arguments for accessibility
g) there are mental barriers and prejudice as well as physical barriers	d) prejudice can be removed by inclusive teaching / more contact / Paralympics & Special Olympics
Conclusion	
c) governments need to do more to reduce physical and mental barriers to inclusion and more diversity	

3 WRITING AN INTRODUCTION

The introduction to the comment should ...

- refer to the topic of the comment — a, b, c
- refer to the cartoon — b, c
- catch the reader's attention — c
- encourage the reader to continue reading — a, c

The most suitable introduction is: c.

4 WRITING A PARAGRAPH

A
b

B
individuelle Lösungen

C
individuelle Lösungen

5 WRITING A CONCLUSION

individuelle Lösungen

8 Multicultural societies

WORKING WITH WORDS

1 WORD FAMILIES: REFUGEE EXPERIENCE

Verb	Adjective	Noun
die	dead, deadly, dying	*death*
endure	*endured, enduring*	*endurance*
fear	*fearful, feared*	fear
persecute	*persecuted, persecuting*	*persecution*
resent	*resentful, resented*	*resentment*
starve	starving, starved	*starvation*
suspect	*suspicious, suspect, suspected*	suspicion
tense	tense	*tension*
threaten	*threatened, threatening*	threat

2 WORD GRID: SYMBOLS AND VALUES

1				S	L	A	V	E	R	Y
2			J	U	S	T	I	C	E	
3	C	H	A	R	I	T	Y			
4		S	P	I	R	I	T			
5				A	R	T	I	S	T	S
6		S	T	A	T	U	E	S		
7			P	R	I	D	E			
8			F	R	E	E	D	O	M	
9			M	E	S	S	A	G	E	

3 ANTONYMS: HUMAN BEHAVIOUR

1 amusement; **2** criticize; **3** nasty; **4** impatient; **5** accept; **6** friendly / reassuring; **7** frown; **8** kindly

GRAMMAR

1 FORMING IF-SENTENCES: TYPE 1

Vorschläge:
If Helmi learns to speak English fluently, he will find a job.
If people become refugees, they will leave their former lives behind.
If people remain in war zones, they will face starvation and violence.
If refugees feel welcome, they will repay locals' kindness.
Locals will be sad to see them go if Helmi and his family return to Syria.
Locals will feel fear and anger if media coverage is negative towards refugees.
The refugee children will soon learn English if they mix with local children.

2 SPOTTING ERRORS: IF-SENTENCES TYPE 2

In Australia many place names are of European origin. ~~You~~ **If you** look at a map of Australia, you **will** find names such as Balmoral, Castlemaine and Hahndorf. For most of these places, Aboriginal names already existed. Other places commemorate 19th-century public figures who were involved in racist practices, such as Macquarie and Mackay. ~~When~~ **If** more people ~~would know~~ **knew** the history, they would understand how offensive these names are. Furthermore, if the Aboriginal place names ~~are~~ **were** widely used, people might become more aware of the indigenous language, culture and history of their area. It would be more difficult for racist attitudes to persist if all Australians **were** ~~will be~~ well informed about their country. However, if everyone agreed that all controversial place names must go, where ~~did~~ **would** it end? [...]

EXAM SKILLS: LISTENING

1 PREPARING TO LISTEN: KEY WORDS

Vorschläge:

1 Australian government, refugee policy, strict(er), relax, change, review
2 ending, boat arrivals, security, danger, ineffective, deaths
3 banning, impossible, situation, plane
4 concern, safety, selfishness, lack of information, propaganda worry
5 illegal, strategy, misunderstanding, law, accurate, understanding
6 arrivals, terrorism, protection, security checks, radicalism
7 strict, regulations, necessary, relaxed, safety, complicated

2 MULTIPLE CHOICE

1b, **2**d, **3**b, **4**a, **5**a, **6**a, **7**c

3 PREPARING TO LISTEN: PREDICTING THE TOPIC

1 A podcast
2 2015 US poll on the Confederate flag
Slogan 'heritage not hate'
African Americans in the Southern states
Use outside the USA
3 racism, civil rights, Southern culture, history, rebellion, extremist symbols, First Amendment, public buildings, official places, National Socialist flag

4 PREPARING TO LISTEN: QUESTIONS

A

1 changing
2 white people
3 people of colour
4 European countries
5 banned

B

1 South Carolina and Mississippi recently stopped using the flag for official purposes. The big supermarket chain Walmart no longer accepts products displaying the flag.
2 White people see it as a symbol of their culture, of which they are very proud.
3 People of colour think that the flag symbolizes racism. It makes them feel unsafe.
4 Far-right groups in Europe use the Confederate flag instead of the Nazi swastika in countries where that symbol is banned,
5 The use of the Confederate flag by private individuals is protected under the First Amendment to the US Constitution.

SKILLS: READING

1 READING FOR GIST

a

2 UNDERSTANDING KEY VOCABULARY

a to dry up: to gradually become less until there is none left
b to reverse: to turn the opposite way around
c prospects: the chances of being successful
d upbeat: positive and enthusiastic
e progress: the process of improving one's situation
f executive: a person who has an important job managing a company
g enclave: an area where people of a different culture live together
h evenly: with equal amounts spread across an area
i root(s): the connections that you have with a place because your family came from there
j to endure: to experience and deal with something that is unpleasant without giving up

3 ANSWERING QUESTIONS

A

Question 1: 2
Question 2: 3
Question 3: 6
Question 4: 7
Question 5: 8
Question 6: 9

B

1 1.5 million eastern Europeans migrated to the UK.
2 Brexit was expected to reverse the migration.
3 The children of the eastern European immigrants are very positive about their future in the UK.
4 The mothers have made more progress in their careers than the fathers.
5 The children have integrated quickly because they have had little contact with other children with their background.
6 The parents worry that the children will forget their own culture.

SKILLS: TRANSLATION

1 DEN TEXT ÜBERFLIEGEN

b

2 VOKABELN MIT MEHREREN ÜBERSETZUNGSMÖGLICHKEITEN

1c, **2**c, **3**c, **4**b

3 FESTSTEHENDE AUSDRÜCKE

1 gewissermaßen, bis zu einem gewissen Grad
2 schließlich, ja
3 infolge von
4 Fuß fassen, sich zurechtfinden
5 gleichzeitig
6 unter Druck stehen

4 ING-FORM

1 Sie haben Schwierigkeiten, *sich zu integrieren.*
2 Es ist wichtig für sie, *ihre Kultur zu behalten.*
3 Es ist ein Mittel, *sich ihre Identität zu erhalten.*

5 DIE ÜBERSETZUNG SCHREIBEN

Die Herausforderungen der Zu-/Einwanderung
Alle europäischen Nationen sind gewissermaßen multikulturell. Heutige Europäerinnen und Europäer sind schließlich das Ergebnis jahrtausendelanger Völkerwanderung. Während der letzten hundert Jahre hat sich die ethnische Zusammensetzung unserer Gesellschaft/Gemeinschaften beschleunigt, da politische und wirtschaftliche Faktoren Millionen von Menschen dazu getrieben haben, ihre Heimat zu verlassen und ein neues Leben und neue Möglichkeiten/Chancen in der Fremde zu suchen.
In dieser Situation/Lage ist ein Aufeinanderprallen der Kulturen wahrscheinlich. Konservative Gemeinschaften stehen neuen Einflüssen misstrauisch gegenüber, sodass Außenseiterinnen und Außenseiter nur schwer Akzeptanz gewinnen. Es hat Fälle gegeben, in denen eine anfängliche freundliche Aufnahme später durch Spannungen und Misstrauen ersetzt wurde, als neue Zuwanderungswellen nachfolgten. Wenn Menschen ihre Lebensweise bedroht sehen, suchen sie oft Sicherheit innerhalb ihrer Gruppe – das gilt sowohl für die Neuankömmlinge als auch ihre Gastgeber. In den schlimmsten Fällen hat dies zu Hass, Gewalt und Verfolgung geführt.
Einwandererinnen und Einwanderer kommen sich in ihrem neuen Land oft schutzlos vor. Einige unter ihnen werden ihre Heimat nur widerwillig verlassen haben, also ist es verständlich, wenn sie damit Schwierigkeiten haben, in einer fremden Umgebung Fuß zu fassen. Während die meisten ihren Gastländern dankbar sind, wollen sie sich aber möglicherweise nicht vollständig in die neue Gesellschaft integrieren. Vielleicht scheitern sie an sprachlichen und kulturellen Barrieren.
Das Festhalten an den Bräuchen und der Kultur des Heimatlandes / Die Bräuche und Kultur des Heimatlandes zu behalten ist eine Mittel/Möglichkeit, sich seine Identität zu erhalten.
Die Kinder dieser Einwanderergeneration tun sich oft schwer, eine eigene kulturelle Identität zu entdecken. Sie erleben Diskriminierungen wegen ihrer Herkunft und werden gleichzeitig von der Familie unter Druck gesetzt, die Kultur ihres Heimatlandes nicht aufzugeben, einschließlich ihrer Religion und Sprache. Möglicherweise fühlen sie, dass sie zu beiden Ländern gehören – oder zu keinem.
Für jede Gesellschaft ist es eine Herausforderung, mit einem tiefgreifenden Wandel fertig zu werden / umzugehen. Andererseits ist der Wandel unvermeidbar: Ist es dann nicht besser, ihm hoffnungsvoll und optimistisch zu begegnen, statt sich gegen ihn zu wehren?

9 The state and politics

WORKING WITH WORDS

1 SOCIETY AND ECONOMICS

1 shortage; **2** retirement; **3** labour; **4** birth; **5** aged; **6** security; **7** career; **8** societal

2 CRIMINAL JUSTICE: VERBS

1 has broken; **2** punishes; **3** protects; **4** guarding; **5** normalizes; **6** discourages; **7** threatening; **8** take; **9** lock; **10** releases; **11** have served; **12** treat; **13** reward; **14** reduces

3 COMPOUND NOUNS

border restrictions; career opportunities; cross-border travel; economic power; labour market; member states; national borders; passport checks; personal freedom

GRAMMAR

1 VERB + INFINITIVE *VS* VERB + -ING

1 having; **2** to stay; **3** dealing; **4** to attract; **5** to reduce; **6** raising; **7** to have; **8** to remain

2 VERB + INFINITIVE *VS* VERB + -ING

to + infinitive:	would prefer, manage, refuse, forget, hope, afford, choose, decide, expect
both:	begin, continue, dislike, hate, like, love, start
-ing:	regret, avoid, consider, deny, enjoy, imagine, miss

3 PRESENT PERFECT AND SIMPLE PAST

1 was; **2** has left; **3** joined; **4** became; **5** came; **6** signed; **7** have joined; **8** have developed; **9** claimed; **10** was; **11** signed / had signed; **12** has always been; **13** agreed; **14** expected; **15** was; **16** voted

EXAM SKILLS: LISTENING

1 PREPARING TO LISTEN: UNDERSTANDING THE GIST

A2, B4, C5, D3, E6, F1

2 MULTIPLE MATCHING

1C, **2**E, **3**A, **4**F Statements not used: B, D

3 PREPARING TO LISTEN: KEY WORDS

Vorschläge:

1 police forces, private businesses, federal, state, guidelines.
2 training, short, skills, military instructors, weapons
3 violent, defend, shoot first, fear, psychological
4 pay, reduced, better job, receive
5 public safety, arresting, police departments, different areas, supportive.
6 social reforms, increase, crime rates, unrelated, idealistic, effective
7 aggressive, violence, harms, communities, expensive, acceptable.

4 MULTIPLE CHOICE

1c, **2**b, **3**c, **4**b, **5**c, **6**d, **7**b

EXAM SKILLS: MEDIATION

1 DIE AUFGABE ANALYSIEREN

Ursprungstext: Armed police: friend or foe?

Mediationstext:

- Adressat: *Mitglieder der Jugendgruppe*
- Medium/Textsorte: *Info-Blatt*
- Zweck: *Informieren über unbewaffnete Polizeistreifen*
- Sprachebene: *informell*

2 DEN INHALT ANALYSIEREN

	A	B	C
Thema	**Absatz**	**Relevanz**	**Bulletpoint**
wie sich US-Polizeistreifen sich Gehorsam verschaffen	10		
Länder, in denen Polizeistreifen unbewaffnet sind	1		
'Policing by consent': Definition	8		2
Vorgehensweise unbewaffneter Streifen bei potenziell gewalttätigen Auseinandersetzungen	9	√	2,3
der leichte Zugang zu Schusswaffen in den USA und dessen Folgen für die Polizei	10	√	3
Verhältnis zwischen Bewaffnung der Polizei u. Waffenkriminalität	2	√	1
Todesfälle-Statistik: Länder mit bewaffneten Polizeistreifen	3, 5	√	1
Todesfälle-Statistik: Länder mit unbewaffneten Polizeistreifen	4	√	1

3 VERFASSEN DER MEDIATION

Lösungsvorschlag / Erwartungshorizont:

a Vorteile unbewaffneter Polizeistreifen:
- weniger Waffenkriminalität
- weniger Todesfälle durch polizeilichen Waffengebrauch
- Statistischer Vergleich mit Ländern mit bewaffneten Polizeistreifen:
  - GB 0–5 Todesopfer jährlich durch polizeilichen Waffeneinsatz
  - Deutschland 10–20 Todesopfer jährlich
  - USA mehr als 1.000 Todesopfer jährlich

b ihre Methoden:
- Deeskalationstraining inkl. Psychologie, Kulturbewusstsein
- verbale Konfliktlösung

c Vorausetzung für den Einsatz von Waffen bei der Polizei:
- wo es absolut nötig sei, z. B. wenn eine Kriminelle eine Waffe bei sich trägt
- in Ländern, wo Waffen frei zugänglich sind

10 A globalized world

WORKING WITH WORDS

1 ADJECTIVE + NOUN COLLOCATIONS

1 raw materials; **2** damning report; **3** backbreaking loads; **4** constant fear; **5** guilty conscience; **6** human rights; **7** illegal miners; **8** moral obligation

2 PREPOSITIONS

1 about, **2** of, **3** in, **4** by, **5** in, **6** with, **7** by, **8** of

3 WORD FAMILIES

A

1 refer
2 familiar
3 economy; economic
4 to grow
5 to advise

B

1 refers
2 familiarize
3 Economists
4 growth
5 advice

GRAMMAR

1 PAST PERFECT AND SIMPLE PAST

1 drove; **2** got; **3** carried; **4** had donated; **5** had driven; **6** had had; **7** had put; **8** said; **9** had been; **10** went; **11** was; **12** had unlocked; **13** came; **14** were; **15** hadn't eaten

2 REPORTED SPEECH: REPORTING VERB IN THE PAST

1 Tina said she **lived** in Duisburg.
2 She said she **didn't work** for a German company.
3 She said she **had worked** for Schmidt KG for 20 years.
4 She said she **had been working** for Wang Ltd for six months.
5 She said she **would stay** at Wang Ltd for the time being.
6 She asked Tim where he **worked**.
7 She asked **if/whether** he **had worked** for a big firm when he lived in London.
8 She asked **if/whether** he **had to** start work early.
9 Tim **asked** Tina **to tell** him about the job interview **the next day**.
10 Tim **told** Tina **not to tell** his boss.

EXAM SKILLS: LISTENING

1 PREPARING TO LISTEN: KEY WORDS

A

Emotions and feelings	People in need	Problems in supermarkets	Supply chain factors
ashamed dignity humiliating proud	children old people refugees single parents	conflict rationing settle disputes shortages	extreme weather conditions human rights political conflicts sustainability

B

a humiliating, **b** refugees, **c** shortages, **d** sustainability

2 MULTIPLE MATCHING

1E, **2**C, **3**B, **4**D   Headings not used: A, F

3 LISTENING FOR INFORMATION

A

1 dying
2 space
3 competition
4 destroying
5 hybrid

B

2, 3

C

1c, 2d, 3b

D

The authorities will process licence applications within days not months.

SKILLS: READING

1 COMPREHENSION

A

1 F, line 1
2 F, line 16
3 T, line 21

B

1 protesters
2 low-skilled
3 developing
4 damage
5 arrested

C

Advantages:
– created wealth
– lifted people out of poverty
– reduced inequality between countries
– boosted economies
– improved the quality of many people's lives

Disadvantages:
– exploited the poor in developing countries
– exploited the low-skilled in advanced economies
– caused environmental damage
– caused the Covid-19 pandemic

D

Lösungsvorschlag:
Visible trade means buying and selling physical products, such as containers of goods, vehicles and machinery. Invisible trade means cross-border data transfers resulting from cloud computing, big data, internet-based services such as social media and e-commerce and foreign direct investment.

E
1 WTO
2 IMF
3 OECD

F

1880–1899	C
1998/9–2007	D
since 2005	B
2008	A

G

1961	The Organisation for Economic Co-operation and Development (OECD) was founded in 1961.
2%	World trade shrank in 2008 after the financial crisis.
20%	Cross-border data transfers have been expanding by up to 20% per year since 2005.

H
- Invisible trade in the form of cross-border data transfers is expanding by 20% per year.
- Foreign direct investment is back to where it was before the financial crisis.

SKILLS: WRITING

1&2
Individuelle Lösungen

3 WRITING THE COMPOSITION

(*Suggested answer*)
Hey Fiona,
I was really interested to hear that you're getting a new smartphone. There are lots to choose from but have you thought about a fair-trade phone? In my opinion, it's important to remember that nowadays, a smartphone is often a fashion accessory or a status symbol because of all the features like fingerprint scanners, etc. The parts and repairs are also expensive and any sign of self-repair voids the guarantee. The result is that we all spend too much money on our phones. Furthermore, there is no guarantee that they are made without child labour and human rights abuses: we shouldn't forget that the workers making them should earn a living wage and live in clean and comfortable accommodation. A fair-trade smartphone guarantees this, you can repair it yourself without special tools and the parts and repairs are affordable. The battery is removable, so you can replace it yourself and it comes with five years' support like most other smartphones. Fair-trade phones are made in safe working conditions using sustainable, low-waste manufacturing technology with recyclable materials and an ethical supply chain.
Best wishes
XX

11 Science and technology

WORKING WITH WORDS

1 OPPOSITES

1 unnecessary; **2** common; **3** false; **4** misleading; **5** huge; **6** private; **7** willing; **8** corrupt; **9** deep; **10** horrified

2 ADJECTIVES FROM NOUNS

A
1 populous; **2** flexible; **3** environmental; **4** psychological; **5** avoidable; **6** erroneous; **7** technological; **8** autonomous; **9** fatal; **10** valuable

B
1 populous; **2** environmental; **3** psychological; **4** fatally; **5** autonomous; **6** flexibly; **7** avoidable; **8** technological

3 WORD FIELD: GENETIC ENGINEERING

1 leukaemia; **2** marrow; **3** diagnosed; **4** treatment; **5** chemotherapy; **6** incurable; **7** palliative care; **8** molecular scissors; **9** infusion; **10** genetically; **11** breakthrough; **12** drug-resistant

GRAMMAR

1 IF-SENTENCES

A

1	will survive	4	wouldn't live
2	don't get	5	wouldn't have cured
3	smoked	6	hadn't given

B
1 hadn't discovered; **2** wouldn't have understood; **3** treat; **4** will survive; **5** had; **6** would make

SKILLS: READING

1 COMPREHENSION

1 The pharmaceutical industry has produced some highly effective vaccines.
2 They were not properly tested; they change your genes; they give you autism.
3 Wear a mask in shops and on public transport; disinfect one's hands regularly; fist-bump instead of shaking hands.
4 350,000 people died of Covid in the USA in one year compared to 25,000 of flu.
5 It carries information to the body's immune system to enable it to combat Covid but dies after a short time because it only survives at low temperatures.
6 The pandemic made it easy to find the large number of people needed for trials.

7 He caught Covid, almost died and now has fatigue, insomnia, no sense of smell and brain fog.

2 MULTIPLE MATCHING

Margaret Trent	F
Ella Jackson	A
Sydney Scott	D
Ted Blunt	B
Headings not used:	C, E

MEDIATION

1 DIE AUFGABE ANALYSIEREN

Ursprungstext: The future of elder care is here – and it's artificial intelligence

Mediationstext:
- Adressat: *Mitschüler/-innen*
- Medium/Textsorte: *Blogpost*
- Zweck: *Darlegen, wie man ältere Menschen mit digitaler Technik zu Hause unterstützen kann*
- Sprachebene: *informell*

2 DEN INHALT ANALYSIEREN

A

a 3
b 2
c 5
d 4, 6, 7
e 2, 5, 8
f 1

B

1 Verhaltensmuster
2 Warnungen
3 abweichen
4 Einwilligung
5 auslösen
6 Verletzung der Privatsphäre
7 vernichtend
8 austricksen

3 VERFASSEN DER MEDIATION

Erwartungshorizont:

Funktionsweise der Alterstechnologie
- Sensoren werden auf Türen und in ausgesuchten Räumen angebracht, um den typischen Tagesablauf der betreffenden Person(en) zu registrieren und zu analysieren. Abweichungen und unerwartete Handlungen werden erkannt und lösen u. U. Warnungen an die pflegende(n) Person(en) aus.

wirtschaftlicher Aspekt
- Mehr Senioren können mit weniger Personal beaufsichtigt werden.

Vorteile
- Senioren haben eine bessere Chance, nicht oder erst später in ein Heim zu kommen.
- Pflegende Angehörige werden entlastet und machen sich weniger Sorgen.
- Angehörige werden automatisch benachrichtigt, wenn die Pflegeperson etwas Unerwartetes macht.
- Die Pflegeperson kann nicht einfach weglaufen und für längere Zeit nicht zurückkommen, ohne das dies erkannt wird.
- Die laufenden Kosten für ein einfaches Überwachungssystem sind nicht hoch.

Nachteile
- Das Überwachungssystem könnte ungenau sein und Trugschlüsse ziehen
- Verletzung der Privatsphäre
- Wissen Senioren, worauf sie sich einlassen, wenn sie ihre Einwilligung geben?
- Sollen ältere Menschen wirklich so leben, d. h. von KI und nicht von Menschen gepflegt werden?
- Das System fördert soziale Isolierung.
- Senioren verhalten sich manchmal unnatürlich, um Warnungen nicht auszulösen oder Verwandte nicht zu belästigen.
- Senioren leiden, weil sie sich ständig unter Beobachtung fühlen und flehen ihre Verwandten an, die Sensoren zu entfernen.
- Einige Senioren sind so einsam, dass sie absichtlich Warnungen auslösen, um eine menschliche Stimme zu hören oder mit jemandem in der Überwachungszentrale einen kleinen Plausch zu halten.

12 The environment

WORKING WITH WORDS

1 VERB + NOUN COLLOCATIONS

A

1 to let in *light*
2 to trap *heat*
3 to support *life*
4 to regulate *the temperature*
5 to save *the world*
6 to tackle *a/the problem*
7 to pass *laws*
8 to generate *electricity*

B

1 regulate the temperature; **2** lets in light; **3** traps the heat; **4** support life; **5** tackle the problem; **6** pass laws

2 WORD FIELD / MIND MAP

1 refuse; **2** litter; **3** reusable; **4** recycling; **5** cleans; **6** volunteers; **7** charge; **8** behavioural; **9** rake; **10** bury; **11** dig; **12** plastic

3 WORD FAMILIES

1 competition; **2** emissions; **3** achieve; **4** self-sufficiency; **5** residents; **6** enthusiastic; **7** resistance; **8** solution; **9** creative; **10** sustainable

GRAMMAR

1 IF-SENTENCES TYPE 1

Vorschläge:
If the rainforests become smaller, there will be more CO_2 in the atmosphere.
There will be more CO_2 in the atmosphere if the rainforests become smaller.
There will be less CO_2 in the atmosphere if the rainforests don't become smaller.
If the rainforests don't become smaller, there will be less CO_2 in the atmosphere.
If the permafrost melts, the buildings on it will collapse.
The buildings on it will collapse if the permafrost melts.
The buildings on it won't collapse if the permafrost doesn't melt.
If the permafrost doesn't melt, the buildings on it won't collapse.
If we protect the coral reefs, coastal communities won't be at risk.
Coastal communities won't be at risk if we protect the coral reefs.
Coastal communities will be at risk if we don't protect the coral reefs.
if we don't protect the coral reefs, coastal communities will be at risk.
If tourists pollute the mangrove swamps, marine, bird, insect and plant life will suffer.
Marine, bird, insect and plant life won't suffer if tourists don't pollute the mangrove swamps,

2 PARTICIPLE CLAUSES

1 Before noticing
2 After seeing
3 since starting
4 after thawing
5 While melting
6 After entering

SKILLS: READING

1 ANALYSING THE TEXT

A 2

B
1 1, 5, 6, 9
2 1
3 5, 6, 7, 8, 9
4 9
5 6
6 7, 8

C
1 New Orleans
2 Kiribati
3 New Orleans
4 Jakarta
5 Humber Estuary, California

2 QUESTIONS ON THE TEXT

1 Humans have pushed back the boundaries of the sea with dikes and reclaimed land or even built artificial islands.
2 They didn't want to leave their homes and communities forever.
3 They had to leave their homes (and run for their lives).
4 They blame the rich countries that caused climate change.
5 They will need to be made higher by digging up sand and rock from the seabed.
6 They bought agricultural land by the rivers.
7 It created wetland areas and wildlife habitats for insects, birds and fish.
8 It is moving its capital elsewhere.

SKILLS: MEDIATION (GERMAN–ENGLISH)

1 ANALYSING THE TASK

original text: Drei große Umweltprobleme, die die Zukunft der Menschheit bedrohen

Mediationstext
- **addressee:** general public, but especially those interested in the environment
- **medium / text type:** blog
- **purpose:** make people aware of challenges facing humanity
- **language register:** neutral

2 ANALYSING THE CONTENT

environmental issues
1 90% of the world's population breathes polluted air
2 over two billion people worldwide do not have safe drinking water
3 food insecurity

what is causing each one
1 world's largest economies still use fossil fuels, coal in particular
2 no access to clean sanitation
3 climate change is causing extreme weather

problems the issue causes
1 breathing difficulties and illness of the lungs
2 illnesses carried through unclean water
3 rise in food prices, food shortages, more under-nourished people

measures that could be taken
1 banning fossil fuels
2 banning the dumping of chemicals in water / investments in water treatment plants
3 eat less animal products; cut food waste

3 WRITING THE MEDIATION

Erwartungshorizont:

the three environmental issues described and what is causing them:

- 90% of the world's population breathes polluted air because the world's largest economies still use fossil fuels, coal in particular.
- Over two billion people worldwide do not have safe drinking water because it is contaminated with faeces. A third of the world's population does not have proper sanitation facilities.
- Climate change is causing food insecurity (is endangering food safety) because extreme weather is harming harvests, water supplies and livestock production.

the problems that they cause for the world's population:

- The air pollution causes breathing difficulties and respiratory illnesses.
- The polluted water spreads disease.
- Food prices will probably rise and there will be food shortages and more undernourished people.

the measures that must be taken.

- Fossil fuels must be banned.
- Dumping chemicals in water must be banned.
- Worldwide and massive investments must be madc water treatment plants.
- The world's population needs to eat far less meat and dairy products and switch to a plant-based diet.
- Food waste must be cut back.
- Food production methods must be sustainable and without pesticides and fertilizer.

SKILLS: TRANSLATION

1 WHETHER

Erwartungshorizont:

1 Haben Sie Ihren Vater gefragt, ob er uns besuchen möchte?
2 Ich frage mich oft, ob der Unfall meine Schuld war.
3 Ich kann mich nicht entscheiden, ob ich bleiben oder gehen soll.
4 Ich konnte mich nicht entscheiden, ob ich bleiben oder gehen sollte.
5 Sie sind sich nicht sicher, ob sie Kinder haben sollen / wollen oder nicht.
6 Sie haben jetzt zwei Wochen Zeit, um zu entscheiden, ob sie das Haus kaufen wollen/sollen oder nicht.

2 MIXED BAG

A

angeben

B

Mehr als die Hälfte der befragten Studentinnen und Studenten gab an, sich vom Umfang des ihnen zugeteilten Lernstoffs überfordert zu fühlen.

3 –ING FORMS

a adjective
b noun
c present progressive
d gerund
e noun
f past progressive (passive)

1 Es gibt alarmierende Anzeichen dafür, dass sich die globale Erwärmung verschlimmert.
2 Sie schloss ihre Aussage mit der Erklärung, dass ihre Gefühle durch seine Haltung ihr gegenüber verletzt würden.

4 DIE UBERSETZUNG SCHREIBEN

Umfrage zeigt Umweltängste bei jungen Menschen auf der ganzen Welt

Eine kürzlich von der Bath University im Vereinigten Königreich durchgeführte Umfrage hat ein alarmierendes Ausmaß an Angst unter jungen Menschen vor dem Klimawandel offenbart. Von den 10.000 Befragten im Alter von 16 bis 25 Jahren aus der ganzen Welt gaben mehr als die Hälfte an, sich traurig, wütend, hilflos und schuldig zu fühlen, und 45 % gaben an, dass ihre Gefühle in Bezug auf den Klimawandel negative Auswirkungen auf ihr tägliches Leben hätten. Drei Viertel hatten Angst vor der Zukunft und fühlten sich von ihren Regierungen betrogen, weil die Politiker zu wenig gegen die globale Erwärmung und ihre Auswirkungen auf den Planeten täten.

Einige waren hoffnungsvoll, aber mehr als die Hälfte glaubte, dass die Menschheit dem Untergang geweiht sei. Ein junger Mensch fasste es zusammen, indem er sagte, dass junge Menschen im Gegensatz zur älteren Generation das Gefühl hätten, dass „die Zerstörung des Planeten etwas Persönliches ist“. Caroline Hickman, die Hauptautorin der Umfrage, erklärte, dass sie nicht nur gemessen habe, was junge Menschen fühlen, sondern auch, was sie denken, und festgestellt habe, dass 40 % der Befragten nicht sicher seien, ob sie Kinder haben sollten oder nicht. Ein junger Mensch sagte: „Ich kann es mir nicht vorstellen, Kinder in einer sterbenden Welt zu bringen.“

Die Forscher waren überrascht über das Ausmaß der Angst, auf das sie stießen, und führten dies teilweise darauf zurück, dass Kinder und Jugendliche sich der Gefahren des Klimawandels sehr wohl bewusst sind, aber praktisch keine Möglichkeit haben, den Schaden zu begrenzen, und daher extrem anfällig für Klimaangst sind.

SKILLS: TEXT PRODUKTION

1 LINKING PHRASES

Vorschläge:

Pollution **is an important issue** all over the world
A case in point is the large accumulation of plastic waste in the Pacific Ocean known as the Great Pacific Garbage Patch.
It must be pointed out that the Pacific is not the only place with a plastic waste problem.
Firstly, the United States generates around 37 million tons of plastic waste each year, **secondly** India generates 9.46 million tons and **thirdly**, China generates 8.8 million tons.
Huge amounts of plastic are used **both / not only** in the construction industry **and / but also** in the packaging industry.
Although Greenpeace has staged dramatic protests / Despite dramatic protests by Greenpeace, including a 10-metre-long plastic monster called Mr Trash Wheel in the Inner Harbor of Baltimore, Maryland in the United States in 2018, the amount of plastic waste in the world's oceans is expected to triple by 2040.
Ultimately, plastic must be replaced by sustainable materials if the problem is to stop growing year by year.

UNIT 6, LISTENING, TASK 2

2

1

For the last half year I've travelled around the UK carrying out 'random acts of kindness.' I like to think that what I do makes people's lives better. Whether I give them a lovely bunch of flowers or pay for their meal in a café – I'm lifting people up. I don't want anything in return. If they want, they can pay it forward – do something nice for another stranger.

My hope is to inspire others through my videos on social media, so that they get out there and make the world a better place. We should all be the change that we want to see in the world, don't you think?

2

There has been a viral spread of 'feel-good' videos lately. They depict people doing nice things for complete strangers. Whether it's hugging people in the street, giving homeless people large amounts of cash or rescuing animals, 'random acts of kindness' are a popular video genre on social media.

When we see stories like this on our social media platforms, we get a warm and fluffy feeling that human beings are really quite nice, after all. Often we click 'share' without much thought – sharing the love. However, if we look a little more closely, these apparently kind actions are not always well received.

3

I didn't want a great bunch of flowers! I was out shopping for my aged Dad, getting a few necessities at the local shopping centre, and I just stopped for a coffee, to relax. I was minding my own business.

I didn't understand at first what on Earth was going on when that boy came up to me and shoved those flowers in my face. Then I saw that his friend was filming the whole thing on her phone!

So, then, later, a friend shared the video with me on social media, saying 'Is this you?' I ... well, I felt that I had been used. I think he was just showing off his generosity – at my expense.

4

There's a huge demand for this kind of content online. 'Love' emojis are the most common reaction to videos on Facebook, according to a massive survey of nearly 800 million posts. Almost half of all posts are 'loved'. The second most common reaction is 'Haha', for a third of posts. 'Sad' and 'angry' emojis together make up only ten per cent.

That tells us a lot about the sorts of videos that social media users want to watch. People want to be delighted, inspired. Problems occur when these 'inspiring' moments are actually set up by influencers – without sufficient thought about the feelings of the ordinary members of the public who are involved.

It's easy to place the blame on influencers, but there's a wider issue. As social media users, shouldn't we be media-savvy enough to recognise when our emotions are being manipulated? And to wonder why?

UNIT 6, LISTENING, TASK 4

3

Narrator:

It all started with annoying ads for a pair of boots. I was seeing these ads everywhere and it was driving me nuts! I vaguely remembered looking at the boots on a shopping website – once.

I decided to do a bit of sleuthing – find out why these ads were following me around the web.

Well, advertising agencies rent space on all the popular websites and social media platforms. Companies offering goods or services pay the agencies to target the people most likely to be interested in their products. So if ten different people visit the same website, they might see ten different ads.

So, why the boots? It turns out that advertisers often use a technique called 'behavioural remarketing'. If you look at a product online but don't buy it the first time, they can 'remind' you to complete the transaction. The idea is that the ad targets people who have shown an interest in a product, instead of advertising to random web users. Makes sense – for the advertisers.

Advertisers use cookies – a simple bit of code fed to the browser by sites that we visit. Cookies are used for a variety of purposes, some of which are useful to you and me. For example, they contain information to make social media or online shopping remember our user preferences and log us in quickly. That's quite convenient.

Other cookies are useful to advertisers, not to us. They enable a site to track our browsing habits, see what we're looking at ... and then they follow us to another site and communicate that information to that site, so that it can serve up suitable ads. That's why they are called 'tracking' cookies. So, I might look at a pair of boots on a shopping website ... then ads for those boots appear on the music streaming service I use, my social media, and so on.

It worried me a little that advertisers were able to track my online behaviour so easily – so I decided to find out what else they might know about me. Here's where it got interesting.

I learned that search engines such as Google monitor our browsing behaviour to build up a profile on us. Terms that we search for are recorded. If we use free online apps, such as text processing, picture editing or email services, our online documents may also be scanned for information useful to advertisers.

I looked at my Google profile and found it had some accurate information about me: my approximate age, income, the part of the world I live in, interests and hobbies, and so on. There are probably a lot of other organisations that have profiled me, holding all kinds of information.

Social media platforms also collect your data. It starts when you sign up and provide information for a user profile. After that, everything you post on social media says something about you: isn't that the point?

Does it matter? Yes, I think it does. It's not just e-commerce companies and their annoying ads. If political organisations know a lot about us, they can manipulate our voting behaviour in specific ways. For example, they can persuade indecisive voters that it's not worth going out to vote at all. That's a threat to democracy, isn't it?

Another thing that worries me is this: if government organisations know a lot about me, they may decide in future to control my behaviour. Our political system is democratic and I trust the authorities with my data – up to a point. However, governments change and can become more authoritarian. Once my data is out there, I can't get it back.

What can I do about it? Not a lot, is my gloomy conclusion. The fact is, if it's online and it's 'free', I'm probably paying for it with my personal data.

If you're determined to do something, you can change your browser settings to reject tracking cookies. Maybe you should avoid services like Google altogether. Use a virtual private network to browse the internet anonymously. Stop using social media.

Alternatively, get on with your life and don't worry about it. How did I make the annoying sneaker ad go away? I just clicked on the 'close' box. A window popped up and I had to select a reason why I didn't want to see this ad anymore. As I closed the window, I reflected: 'Well, that's even more information I've just given the advertisers ...'

UNIT 8, LISTENING, TASK 2

4

Haasim
My parents came here as refugees, from Lebanon, but we've got to have rules. People who arrive illegally, by boat, without a visa, they've got to be told that they won't be allowed to settle in Australia – ever.

When the government brought in its 'offshore processing' policy and decided that arrivals by sea would never be allowed to settle in Australia, it was the right thing to do. Both sides of politics agreed with it.

I know, I know – it seems harsh, but it has saved hundreds of lives. Look at the illegal arrivals from Indonesia. These people, I understand that they were desperate to get here, but they were putting themselves at risk. The boats they came in were overcrowded and unsafe. Hundreds crammed in tiny little fishing boats! It was dangerous and it needed to stop. Look how many drowned at sea.

Beth
Hi, Beth here, from Sydney. Look, people who want to ban arrivals by boat just aren't living in the real world. Don't they realise that a lot of refugees don't even have travel documents, so they can't just go to an airport and get on a plane?

I've heard this 'concern' about safety so many times, as an argument against allowing boat arrivals in, and ... it's totally, completely insincere. They're always so 'concerned' about refugees drowning at sea on their way to Australia, right? Yeah, but they're never concerned enough to ask our government to send navy ships – or even cruise ships – to Indonesia to pick up the displaced people and bring them to Australia in comfort and safety, are they? No.

They're never 'concerned' about the safety of the refugees while they're being persecuted in their home countries, or stuck for years in transit camps in other poor countries, with no rights and no future. All they're really 'concerned' about is themselves, when it comes down to it.

Kon
G'day. I'm Kon, from Perth, and I'm proud to be a refugee advocate. Let's be clear: Australia has signed up to the UN International Conventions on Refugees and there is absolutely *nothing* in those treaties which requires refugees to have travel documents or to settle in the first country they enter after leaving their home country. It is a fundamental human right to seek asylum in the face of persecution.

Politicians who call arrivals by boat 'illegal' are making up their own rules, so that they can feel good ... about a selfish and inhumane policy. They should know better and in fact mostly they *do* know better. They're just picking on the weakest people in our society in the name of their own political advantage.

We have a term for that in Australia: 'dog whistling' – in other words, appealing to people's worst instincts. We ought to be better than that.

Marysa
I'm worried that letting in people without proper approval procedures will mean that terrorists can get into our country, posing as refugees. Remember that these people are often coming to Australia from very violent environments. They may come from war zones, or from countries which have a lot of political and religious radicalism.

I'm all for helping people in need, but there have to be proper procedures and an orderly queue – not just push your way in. At the end of the day, we have a right to decide who enters our country and who stays. We need to protect our borders and our national security.

UNIT 8, LISTENING, TASK 4

5

Host The use of the Confederate flag in America today is controversial. To some Americans it represents pride in Southern heritage, to others it signifies white supremacy and celebrates slavery, racism and oppression. Who is right? With me in the studio to discuss this is Alice Wheeler, curator of the Southern Heritage Museum in Georgia.

Wheeler Hello!

Host And on the phone link is Felicity Jones, a historian and civil rights advocate from Cleveland, Ohio.

Jones Hi!

Host Ms Jones, if I may turn to you first?

Jones Please do.

Host Public opinion is divided: in a national survey back in 2015, a majority of Americans thought that the Confederate flag represented Southern pride rather than racism. What do you think of that?

Jones It was a narrow majority, 57 per cent. And the times are changing, fast. South Carolina and Mississippi recently stopped using the flag for official purposes, and the big supermarket chain Walmart no longer accepts products displaying it.

Host Where do you stand personally, Ms Jones? Is the flag racist, in your view?

Jones I'd say that its connection with racist politics can't be denied. During the 1948 United States presidential election it was used by the Dixiecrats, a political party that opposed civil rights to African Americans and supported racial segregation. After that, it was used by opponents of the Civil Rights Movement.

Host Ms Wheeler, what do you say to that?

Wheeler Well, I'd like to point out that the Confederate battle flag was also used by the New Left anti-racist movement in the 1960s and 1970s ...

Host This is all history. What does the flag mean to Americans now? Ms Wheeler?

Wheeler There's an expression that we use a lot in the South – 'heritage not hate'. I think that sums up how we feel about it in the South. We're proud of our culture, and the flag is a symbol of that.

Host Ms Jones?

Jones That's what Southern white people might say, but if you ask Southern people of colour, you get a different story. Going back to those poll results that were mentioned earlier: the Southern states yielded a completely different result to the country as a whole. Seventy-five per cent of Southern black people said the flag symbolised racism. They were quite clear about that.

You can't ignore history. What happened in the past affects us right now. Symbols like the Confederate battle flag don't lose their old meanings. It's a flag which makes people of colour feel unsafe. And for good reason.

Wheeler Symbols can take on new meanings, alongside the old ones. For many people, the Confederate flag is a light hearted symbol of 'rebellion' without any significant political meaning.

Jones Well, let's talk how the flag is being used right now, shall we? If you look at far-right groups in Europe, they use it alongside the Nazi swastika, or instead of the swastika where that symbol is banned, so they clearly understand its racist symbolism.

Host Is it time to ban the Confederate flag, then? Find another symbol for Southern pride?

Wheeler There is no question of banning the flag. Its use by private individuals is protected under the First Amendment.

Jones As are, for example, the flags of the Third Reich and other far-right extremist symbols. That doesn't mean that we need to endorse it officially by using it on our public buildings – or our license plates.

Host I'm afraid that's all we have time for. Ms Jones, Ms Wheeler, thank you for this interesting debate.

UNIT 9, LISTENING, TASK 2

6

1

Host More than three-and-a-half million children are living below the poverty line in the UK. That's one of the worst child poverty rates in the industrialized world. Poverty is not just a matter of not having enough money to make ends meet. It puts young people at risk in a multitude of ways.

Statistics show a strong correlation between poverty and asthma for example. Nearly half of children with asthma belong to the poorest 10 per cent of families in the UK. A staggering 85 per cent of children who live in damp houses suffer from asthma or other respiratory problems.

On today's programme, three English teenagers describe what it's like, growing up in a family that's always short of cash. Taylor is seventeen, he has lived in a high-rise flat in Liverpool nearly all his life. Harry, also seventeen, lives with his father in Bristol. Sixteen year-old Caitlyn, from Bradford, lives with her mother and two sisters.

2

Taylor This place really is a dump! Me and me friends used to find needles in the street where we were playing – it's not very nice to see that when you go out to play ... but the main problem is our flat.

These flats were built in the 1970s. They were a quick, cheap solution to housing a lot of people. But they skimped on quality, and fifty years later – they need pulling down, to be honest. The council made some improvements a few years ago – but they were mostly cosmetic. Pretty the place up on the outside to hide the problems!

Our flat has damp all over the walls. It looks a mess, but there isn't much Mum and Dad can do. They tried putting wallpaper and paint on it but the damp just came through. It smells horrible too. It's disgusting here and we feel sick all the time. The doctor reckons that's where my asthma comes from.

3

Harry I used to have a lot of problems with bullying at school. When you can't afford nice clothes like everyone else, you stand out. Even though we all had to wear school uniform – everyone could tell who the poor kids were, in second-hand uniforms. I always tried to stay in the background, cos I didn't want people to know what my home life was like, but it didn't help. I started skipping school whenever I could, just to avoid the stress of it all.

I saw a show on TV that said a lot of poor children have thoughts about suicide, and I have to admit, I had stuff like that going around in my head when I was younger. I blamed myself for my family's situation, see. I was thinking stuff along the lines of 'Nobody wants me here. Dad would be better off without me.'

I don't think that way now so much, but it still makes me angry that my dad can't find a job. They say the economy's improving, but we aren't seeing it around here.

4

Caitlyn For tea we just have, like, a meat pie or maybe a sausage roll each. It's not really enough, but it's all that Mum can afford to put on the table, with three teenage girls in the house. During term time, we get free dinners at school, so that helps. Often school dinner's the only decent meal we get all day. Yeah, but in the holidays, Mum really struggles to feed us properly. We do what we can to help out with the money situation, but it's not enough.

From science classes at school I know that what we eat isn't good for us. It's unhealthy. It's basically just junk food – but it's cheap and it's filling. You've got to take what you can get, haven't you? Better than going hungry.

UNIT 9, LISTENING, TASK 4

7

Host Welcome to the American Dialogues podcast. I'm your host, Susannah Keyes ...

Today our topic is 'Reimagining the police.' Police forces across the USA have a problem, and it's no secret. In recent years there has been a spate of high-profile cases where police have been alleged to use excessive force against unarmed members of the public. Offiers have been convicted for murder and lesser crimes.

There are loud voices demanding reform. The demands range from better police training through to 'defunding' and even 'abolishing' the police.

Troy Rivers, you're an ex-police officer who's in favour of reforming the police. Why is that?

Troy Thank you, Susannah. There are over 18,000 different law enforcement agencies across the USA. Let that sink in for a moment. Eighteen thousand. Police departments are largely organised on a local or state level. Training is not standardised. This mess needs to be cleaned up: fewer police forces, better training.

Host What's wrong with police training?

Troy It all starts with a recruit's basic training – training which tends to address the wrong areas. It's a military-type training. The trouble is, police aren't supposed to be soldiers, and the public aren't supposed to be the enemy.

Host That's a strong statement. Can you back it up with some facts?

Troy Sure. On average, a raw recruit spends 21 weeks in training before going on patrol as a rookie officer, armed with a gun and authorised to use deadly force. Of the 630 or so hours of training that the recruit receives, around 20 hours is about dealing with the public. Twenty hours.

Host That doesn't seem like much ...

Troy It isn't. It includes about six hours of training in cultural competency, seven hours of training in communication skills and five hours of training in ethics. Most of the rest of the training – over 600 hours – focuses on things like report writing, driving skills, patrol procedures, criminal law and firearms training. Remember, these are averages. There are officers out there with a lot less training than this.

Host I see. How might police training be different?

Troy In many ways. One example is de-escalation training. Using psychology to defuse dangerous situations, calm angry and potentially violent people, persuade them to comply with instructions. This requires a lot more work on communication skills, cultural skills and practical psychology. It's actually the opposite of what many US police officers are trained to do. They learn to escalate the threat of violence until the person complies – or violence is used. The results speak for themselves.

Host Alicia Morales, you are a member of an LA-based activist group advocating defunding the Los Angeles Police Department. Are you an anarchist?

Alicia Not at all. I'm in favour of good government and improving public safety.

Host So how is defunding the police a solution? That seems to be counter-intuitive. We should be spending *more* on policing if we want to be safer, surely?

Alicia There simply isn't enough money to do that. In most cities across the USA, policing is already the biggest expense. It costs $1.8 billion to fund the LA police, for example, that's nearly 20 per cent of the city budget.

Host Okay, but I still don't understand how taking money away from the police would help.

Alicia We don't just want to take money away from them and leave them to do the same tasks with fewer resources, that would be crazy. We want to spend the money on improving public safety in other ways.

Host How do you mean?

Alicia We believe that this money would be better spent on supporting people, rather than arresting them.

Host That sounds a little idealistic, if you don't mind my saying ...

Alicia No, it's based on evidence. We can better support young people by opening new youth centres. We can better assist people with mental illnesses by improving mental health services. We can reduce domestic violence by providing more counselling services – and vital emergency accommodation for women and children at risk. More broadly, we can invest more in community infrastructure, like employment, housing and education. Those things have been proven, around the world, time after time, to reduce crime.

Host And deploying more police officers doesn't reduce crime?

Alicia Sending in heavily armed police officers almost never reduces criminal activity in the long term. It creates fear and distrust and harms community relations. Dysfunctional communities are precisely the places where crime flourishes.

Host Troy, Alicia – thank you for your contributions. And thank you to everyone out there for listening in. Until next time!

UNIT 10, LISTENING, TASK 2

8

1

As a supermarket manager, I hate gaps on the shelves. Once we could rely on last-minute deliveries of goods from all over the world thanks to globalization, but those days are gone. Nowadays there are shortages. Shortages of flour, cooking oil, pasta, even toilet paper. And when the goods finally arrive, we have to ration them. Rationing at the checkout! How ridiculous! One pack of toilet rolls per customer and no more! One bottle of cooking oil only! And that's when the next problem starts: the manager as mediator. I get called in to mediate in a conflict between an old-age pensioner and a young mother, fighting over a bottle of cooking oil. I wasn't trained to settle disputes. I was trained to sell but now I actually have to prevent customers from buying goods!

2

Globalization? I'm not sure what that means. I'm a pensioner, I'm 68 years old, I left school at 16 and worked all my life as a maintenance man and caretaker until I retired at 65. I was proud of never being unemployed and now ... now I can't afford a bottle of cooking oil! It's humiliating. I never thought I would end up poor. Poverty is a terrible thing. You feel ashamed and try to hide it. My wife and I live off a fixed income and if the prices go up, we feel the pain. Perhaps it's because of globalization, but I say it's about dignity. Nowadays we have to think twice before we buy any extras. Flowers on the kitchen table and a pint in the pub make a big difference if you've got the money.

3

As a buyer for a large retail organization my job is all about sourcing. I look for suppliers who can deliver goods on time and within budget. When the world was a global village, we could go anywhere for our goods, as long as the suppliers met our criteria, which were no child labour, no slave wages, no human rights abuses, no animal testing and, of course, sustainability. But now we have a new problem: global supply chain disruption. Long supply chains are vulnerable to extreme weather conditions, vulnerable to labour shortages and lockdowns, vulnerable to political conflicts and, of course, vulnerable to war, which changes everything. We need to think small and think local and be more flexible, more agile and better able to improvise to handle the challenges of the future.

4

I run a food bank and we get all sorts in here. Some you would expect, like single parents with young children who can't earn enough to feed their families. 30 per cent of the people we feed are children but recently there's been a surge of 20 per cent in the numbers of old people with a small pension who just can't make ends meet. Do I believe this has anything to do with globalization? I would say yes, mainly because of inflation. We get most of our food from discounters and supermarkets that donate unsold goods to us. Now however, with global inflation, they are ordering less and throwing away less. At the same time the price of everything is going up, electricity, gas, oil and heating, not just food. And then there are the refugees. Things are not looking good.

UNIT 10, LISTENING, TASK 3

9

Interviewer Hello and welcome to *Sophie Winter Live.* Today my studio guest is Thomas Link, the new local mayor. Welcome to the show, Thomas, and thank you very much for agreeing to take part in a question and answer session about what is happening to the town centre.

Mayor My pleasure, Sophie.

Interviewer So could you first just describe the situation in the town centre for our listeners in a few words?

Mayor Yes, certainly, Sophie. The fact of the matter is that the town centre is dying. More and more shops, restaurants and cafés are closing down and none are opening to take their place. I've lived here all my life and what was once a busy town centre full of people young and old is now very often just an empty space. It's heart-breaking and I intend to do something about it.

Interviewer Thanks for that, Thomas. But before we hear what you have in mind, let me explain to our listeners that before this programme, we asked people in the street to give us their theories and ideas about what is going wrong, so that you, Thomas, as the mayor of the town, can respond to them. One of the reasons given was globalization. Shops are closing because of global online competition and we here in this town are in fact competing with a global giant based in the US and can never win.

Mayor Yes, there is global competition online and yes, one big platform is destroying physical shops, but the answer is for shops to offer a hybrid service with both offline and online sales.

Interviewer And who will host their websites, the global online giant? That would be counter productive.

Mayor Exactly, and that's why I intend to help set up a regional online sales platform for local businesses, so they can all help each other.

Interviewer A regional sales platform certainly sounds like a great idea, but I have another reason given for empty shops in the town centre and that is that the rents are too high and the rental periods are too long.

Mayor I'm delighted that you've mentioned this problem, Sophie, because you're absolutely right. We are living in troubled times, and no one wants to sign a contract for five years and pay a high rent. I plan to talk to the owners of the commercial premises in the town centre and encourage them to do three things. One, make the rents lower; two, make the minimum rental periods shorter, by which I mean 12 months and not five years; three, make the shops smaller. The days of big department stores are over. We need smaller units.

Interviewer I'm sure potential retailers will be pleased to hear that, Thomas. Now, another comment we heard was that town centres all look the same because they all have the same chain stores and fast food restaurants. What do you say to that?

Mayor I say that's a pretty fair description. There's no variety at the moment but one way to change things is to allow pop-up shops, so retailers can experiment with new ideas.

Interviewer That sounds promising, but now let's move on to another problem in town and city centres: too many fast-food snack bars and restaurants producing too much plastic litter.

Mayor Well, as regards the snack bars we have to think big. My research team asked younger people who do a lot of computer work whether they preferred to work at home or in the office. The answer was surprising, because over a third prefer working in coworking spaces and cafés. This is because they want both company and freedom at the same time.

Interviewer I see, but could you just explain to our listeners what a coworking space is?

Mayor Yes, of course. A coworking space is a central office location where people can rent a place to sit and work by the day, week, month or longer. It has the basics such as desks, Wi-Fi and printers and perhaps also a conference room. People doing different work share the same facilities and, of course, there has to be a café nearby. We want to offer such facilities in the town centre to encourage people back into town and are in negotiations with the owners of commercial premises.

Interviewer And the plastic litter? How will you get rid of all the disposable, throw-away plastic packaging?

Mayor We plan to tax fast-food outlets using throw-away plastic packaging. We have a statistic on that and 29 per cent of the retailers we asked believe that disposable and non-recyclable packaging should be taxed. A few years ago it was zero, so retailers are beginning to understand that they must stop selling their goods in throwaway plastic packaging.

Interviewer I think we have time for one more comment. One of the people asked in the street said the town centre is boring in the evening and at weekends. How can it be made more attractive?

Mayor My team has done some background research into this problem and found out that at least 32 per cent of people like going out to pubs and restaurants once or twice a month. At the moment, there is little to encourage them to go into a dead town centre in the evenings, but my team and I are going to make it easier for new restaurants, cafés and pubs to get catering licences.

Interviewer And how will you do that?

Mayor Well, currently it takes months to process an application for a catering licence and it involves a lot of complicated bureaucracy and form-filling. If we, the authorities, offer help to the applicants and process their applications much more quickly, and by that I mean in days and not in months, this will encourage people to open new premises and give the town centre a new look.

Interviewer Well, our time's up and I think our listeners will agree that you, Thomas, and your team have some exciting ideas to help the town centre come back to life again. Thanks for coming on the show and, of course, a big thanks to our listeners for tuning in. We'll be back next week at the same time, so don't miss the next episode of *Sophie Winter Live* ...

6th edition

FOCUS on success

ALLGEMEINE AUSGABE

Workbook mit Skills Training

und Lösungsbeileger

von
James Abram
Michael Benford
Steve Williams

Unter Mitarbeit der Verlagsredaktion

Audios online verfügbar unter
www.cornelsen.de/webcodes. **Code: puwodi**

Cornelsen

CONTENTS

UNIT	WORKING WITH WORDS	GRAMMAR
FOUNDATION COURSE		
1 HOLIDAYS AND TOURISM	activities and holidays; safari tour	word order; personal pronouns and possessive adjectives; simple present *vs* present progressive
2 ADVENTURE SPORTS	word field: sports; words that are easily confused	simple past; present perfect with *since* or *for*; simple past *vs* present perfect
3 MY IMAGE, MY STYLE	body image: verbs; body image: collocations; word formation	some, any, much, many, a lot of; few, little, lot(s), much; uncountable nouns
4 STRESS AND PRESSURE	word field: Suneung; word formation; phrasal verbs	adjectives and adverbs; comparing adjectives and adverbs
MAIN COURSE		
5 MY WORKING LIFE	collocations with 'job'; noun collocations; word formation	the future: simple present and present progressive; *will* future and *going-to* future; the future: mixed tenses
6 CONNECTED WORLDS	collocations and compounds; social media adjectives; correct word	the passive: spotting and correcting errors; the passive: completing sentences
7 DIVERSITY IN SOCIETY	idiomatic verb phrases; word families; word building	simple past and past progressive; modal verbs, relative clauses
8 MULTICULTURAL SOCIETIES	word families: refugee experience; word grid: symbols and values; antonyms: human behaviour	forming if-sentences: type 1; spotting and correcting errors: if-sentences type 2;
9 THE STATE AND POLITICS	society and economics; criminal justice: verbs; compound nouns	verb + infinitive *vs* verb + -ing; present perfect and simple past
10 A GLOBALIZED WORLD	adjective + noun collocations; prepositions; word families	past perfect and simple past; reported speech: reporting verb in the past
11 SCIENCE AND TECHNOLOGY	opposites; adjectives from nouns; word field: genetic engineering	if-sentences
12 THE ENVIRONMENT	verb + noun collocations; word field; word families	if-sentences type 1; participle clauses
TRACKS UND QUELLEN		

BUILDING SKILLS (FC) / SKILLS (MC)	PAGE
preparing to read	4
dealing with unknown words	7
reading for gist	10
analysing statistics	13
Reading: 'Britain's hidden online 'microworkers' paid less that £4 an hour' Writing: a discussion	16
Listening: Random acts of kindness Listening: Tracking advertisements Mediation (English–German): Bursting the bubble Analysing a cartoon	22
Reading: 'UK schools warned not to ban afro hairstyles' Writing: a comment	30
Listening: Attitudes towards refugees in Australia Listening: US Americans discuss the Confederate flag Reading: 'Changing Nation' Translation (English–German): 'The challenges of immigration'	36
Listening: Childhood poverty in the UK Listening: The police in the USA Mediation (English–German): 'Armed police: friend or foe?'	44
Listening: Globalization Listening: The town centre Reading: 'Globalization RIP – Long live globalization!' Writing: An email	50
Reading: 'Are anti-vaxxers a thing of the past? British reporter Toby Simpson toured the US to find out' Mediation (English–German): 'The future of elder care is here – and it's artificial intelligence'	58
Reading: 'Mass migration on the horizon' Mediation (German–English): 'Drei große Umweltprobleme, die die Zukunft der Menschheit bedrohen' Translation (English–German): 'Survey reveals eco-anxiety in young people across the world' Writing: Linking phrases	64
	80

1 Holidays and tourism

WORKING WITH WORDS

1 ACTIVITIES AND HOLIDAYS

» SB, S6

A Complete the gaps in the 'Activities' column with suitable verbs from the list. You need some words more than once.

do • go • have • hitchhike • lie • relax • see • sleep • stay • travel

	Activities		Type of holiday
1	________ at home	________ on your balcony	________
2	________ canyoning	________ something exciting	________ holiday
3	________ in a tent	not ________ in hotels	________ holiday
4	________ new sights	________ a wonderful time	________ holiday
5	________ in the sun	________ nothing	________ holiday
6	________ around Europe	________ by train	________ holiday

B Now add the type of holiday in the right-hand column.

2 SAFARI TOUR

» SB, S7–11

Which words are missing from the Solisi Safari Tours information & checklist?

		Tour information & checklist
1	*Tour operator*	*Solisi Safari Tours Ltd*
2	________	*Kruger National Park, South Africa*
3	________	*Liese (tour guide), Thabo (safari guide)*
4	________	*Explorer trucks*
5	________	*comfortable tents on campsites*
6	Washing ________	*bathrooms and washrooms at campsites*
7	________	*savanna landscape and 'Big Five' wild animals in their natural habitat*
8	Meals and ________	*meals included, drinks not included*
9	________	*sockets at campsites, pack portable charger!*
10	________	*cash for drinks and souvenirs, credit card in Johannesburg*
11	Visa ________	*check with SA embassy for latest information*
12	________	*check with family doctor if necessary*
13	________	*not included, buy from a travel agent!*

GRAMMAR

1 WORD ORDER

>> SB, GF19, S269

Write at least six sentences in your exercise book using words and phrases from the table below.

signal words	place	time	activity
always • never • often • regularly • sometimes • usually	Italy • Spain • Austria • at home • at the beach • in London	in August • after Easter • at the weekend • in the summer holidays • for the whole of July • during the summer	go camping • take a sightseeing trip • relax on the beach • stay • go backpacking • go skiing

Jonah sometimes stays at home in the summer holidays.

2 PERSONAL PRONOUNS AND POSSESSIVE ADJECTIVES

>> SB, S9

Complete these dialogues with the missing words.

1 **A** Hi, Becky. Hi, Simon. Have ________ got a portable charger? I can't find ________ charger anywhere. Maybe ________ lost ________ somewhere.
B Hi, Lauren. Sure, ________ can borrow ________ charger. ________ aren't using it right now.

2 **A** Kip took ________ to see a family of lions yesterday. ________ said ________ were really difficult to find.
B I'd love to have ________ job. ________ spends all ________ time with wild animals.

3 **A** I hate this campsite! ________ washing facilities aren't as clean as the others. I don't like using ________ at all.
B What does Deanna say? I think ________ should all complain to ________ about ________.

4 **A** Hi, Lauren. Could ________ take a photo of the two of ________? We want to send ________ to our grandchildren. So ________ can see what ________ grandparents are doing on safari.

3 SIMPLE PRESENT *VS* PRESENT PROGRESSIVE

>> SB, S9+11–12; GF1–2, S258

Complete this travel blog with the correct form of the verb in brackets.

I ________________ [1] (not like) flying because I ________________ [2] (think) it's really bad for the environment, so I usually ________________ [3] (stay) at home during the summer holidays. I always ________________ [4] (find) lots of interesting things to do at home and I ________________ [5] (love) going hiking in the mountains near my home town. A couple of friends ________________ [6] (come) and visit me regularly, and they often ________________ [7] (say) what a good idea a staycation is. But right now, I ________________ [8] (take) my summer holiday in Venice. I ________________ [9] (sit) in a café in St Mark's Square and ________________ [10] (watch) all the tourists who ________________ [11] (enjoy) the city like me. At the moment, the sun ________________ [12] (shine) but people ________________ [13] (stand) in 20cm of water from the lagoon. This ________________ [14] (be) Venice, folks! Who would have thought it? The one summer when I ________________ [15] (decide) to go to Venice, there has to be a huge flood. Today, everyone ________________ [16] (wear) macs and rubber boots, but the queue to get into St Mark's Cathedral ________________ [17] (not be) shorter than usual. And the tour buses and cruise ships ________________________ [18] (still/pour) out hundreds of tourists every day into the city. The only difference is that people ________________ [19] (have to) register online before they can enter the city.

BUILDING SKILLS

PREPARING TO READ

» SB, S12–13; SF4, S238

A Quickly read the title and introduction of the following newspaper article and tick what you think the text will be about.

a popular holiday destinations for young people ☐
b how social media influences holiday choices ☐
c the top 5 holiday destinations on social media ☐

Social media 'ruining vacations', says report

Instagrammability of destination is the top priority for Millennials and Gen Z when choosing a holiday destination.

[1] According to research carried out on behalf of travel website GoWorld, two-thirds of millennials and Gen Z-ers stated that they were inspired to choose a travel destination based on how it would look on their social media channels. The results come as no surprise considering the rise in social media influencers sponsored to travel to exotic places and post enviable pictures.

[2] And when Millennials travel, you can assume they will be posting photos of beautiful beaches or romantic sunsets – but not for the reason you may think. Rather than uploading images on social media as virtual memories to look back on fondly, social media users are mostly posting their vacation snaps to incite envy among their friends and followers, according to the survey. Roughly 20 per cent of men surveyed, and 10 per cent of women, admitted that they would even go so far as to post fake holiday photos to social media.

[3] But it turns out that real life is not the same as social media, as many holidaymakers have found out post-vacation. According to GoWorld, one in five Millennials and Gen Z-ers felt disappointed by a famous location when compared to Instagram. The top letdowns according to the research were all iconic landmarks: Sydney Opera House, the Spanish Steps in Rome, the Taj Mahal, Stonehenge and Times Square. (237 words)

B Use the 'traffic light reading' strategy (SB, page 238) to mark or highlight words in the text.

C Skim (SB, page 239) the text, then match paragraphs 1–3 to the correct content (a–d). There is one more item of content than you need.

a Many Millennials and Gen Z-ers choose travel destinations based on how they will look on social media channels. ___
b Many tourist sights are disappointing compared to social media photos. ___
c Men are more likely than women to choose a holiday destination according to its Instagrammability.. ___
d Photos are posted on social media to impress family and friends. ___

D Now scan (SB, page 239) the text and note down the following information:

1 the number of Millennials and Gen Z-ers who choose holidays based on their suitability for social media

______

2 the reason why social media has become so important for holiday destinations

______

3 the reason why Millennials and Gen Z-ers post photos of their holidays

______

4 the number of men and women who might post fake holiday photos

______

2 Adventure sports

WORKING WITH WORDS

1 WORD FIELD: SPORTS

» SB, S15

A Find eight more sports in the word puzzle – and the names of the places where you do each sport. The answer words are vertical, horizontal or diagonal and read in any direction.

S	X	T	R	A	K	T	M	N	P	G	Q	W	X	Y
C	P	O	I	C	J	E	H	G	N	O	R	X	C	E
I	Q	W	A	E	R	N	T	I	Z	L	U	I	P	O
T	D	R	S	D	F	N	R	G	H	F	J	K	L	V
E	T	N	Y	P	X	I	C	E	H	O	C	K	E	Y
L	C	V	O	B	O	S	N	M	Q	W	E	R	T	Z
H	U	I	P	M	C	O	S	W	I	M	M	I	N	G
T	P	A	S	O	A	D	L	F	G	T	H	N	K	N
A	Q	I	U	W	E	I	R	T	R	Z	U	K	A	I
S	D	R	T	F	G	H	D	U	J	K	Y	X	C	X
V	S	B	N	C	F	O	O	T	B	A	L	L	M	O
E	M	Y	C	V	H	C	L	L	A	B	E	S	A	B

B In your exercise book, write down two pieces of equipment or clothing you need to do each sport.

2 WORDS THAT ARE EASILY CONFUSED

» SB, S15–18

Circle the most suitable verb to complete the sentences.

1 Luisa plays / goes football twice a week. Her father practices / trains her team.

2 She also does / goes parkour with her friend Matty and sometimes they do / go mountain biking in the woods.

3 Luisa had / made an accident recently. She fell / jumped off her bike when she hit / beat a rock with her front wheel.

4 Fortunately, Luisa didn't break / hurt her ankle, but it is still very painful.

5 It hasn't stopped her from practising / training some new parkour moves. Matty is learning / teaching her how to do a somersault.

6 She loves playing / performing her parkour moves when her friends are watching. They don't mind if she does / makes a mistake.

7 Luisa becomes / gets a tingling feeling when she is doing parkour. 'If you want to live / survive in this sport, you have to pay / spend attention to the details,' she says.

GRAMMAR

1 SIMPLE PAST

>> SB, S16; GF3, S259

Complete the sentences with the correct simple past form of the verbs in brackets.

Ella Van Sant ______________ [1] (make) her first BASE jump when she ______________ [2] (be) just 16 years old. She and her friends ______________ [3] (drive) to the Snake River Canyon in Idaho. They ______________ [4] (go) there at night so that nobody could see what they were doing. Ella ____________________ [5] (not jump) straight away. Her friends ______________ [6] (have) to count down three times before she finally ______________ [7] (take) the plunge and ______________ [8] (throw) herself off the bridge. She ______________ [9] (know) as soon as her parachute ______________ [10] (open) that she had found the right sport for her. 'BASE jumping ______________ [11] (teach) me to live my life to the full,' she said.

2 PRESENT PERFECT WITH *SINCE* OR *FOR*

>> SB, S17–18; GF5, S259

Complete the sentences with the correct present perfect form of the verbs in brackets. Add *since* or *for* wherever necessary.

1 Bob Meads ____________________ (teach) BASE jumpers ______________ over 15 years.
2 He ____________________ (do) over 1000 jumps ______________ he first started BASE jumping.
3 Naomi Osaka ____________________ (be) a professional tennis player ______________ September 2013.
4 She was born in Japan in 1997, but she ____________________ (live) in the USA ______________ 2000.
5 Ella Van Sant and her friends ____________________ (not jump) anywhere ______________ over a week.
6 They ____________________ (have) bad colds ______________ a couple of days.

3 SIMPLE PAST *VS* PRESENT PERFECT

>> SB, S17–18; GF3+5, S259

Complete the article with the correct form of the verb in brackets. Use the simple past or the present perfect. Add *since* or *for* wherever necessary.

A mountain rescue team ____________________ [1] (answer) an SOS call in the Canadian Rocky Mountains yesterday after a wingsuit flyer ____________________ [2] (get) into difficulties on Mount Orion.
'I ________________ [3] (be) with this team ________________ [4] over 10 years, but I ________________ [5] (never / see) anything as scary – or funny – as this,' ____________________ [6] (say) rescue team leader, Jake Clement. The wingsuit flyer ____________________ [7] (survive) a 100m fall after he ____________________ [8] (fall) over before he could even start his jump. His wingsuit ____________________ [9] (catch) in some trees which ____________________ [10] (stop) him from falling to his death 2500m below. The size of the suit, however, ____________________ [11] (mean) that he wasn't able to free himself.
'We ____________________ [12] (laugh) when we first saw him, but this ____________________ [13] (be) one of the most difficult rescues I ______________________________________ [14] (ever – take) part in,' Clement ________________ [15] (comment). The number of rescue calls ____________________________ [16] (go up) sharply ____________________ [17] 2020. According to Clement, Mount Orion ______________________________ [18] (become) a hot-spot for accidents.

BUILDING SKILLS

>> SB, S17; SF1, S232

DEALING WITH UNKNOWN WORDS

A Analyse the meaning of the highlighted words by breaking them down into the original word, prefix and suffix (where possible). Give the word form of the new word and its meaning.

Nature Watch criticizes unacceptable damage to mountain

Coexistence of BASE jumpers and nature lovers on popular jumping hotspot

The peaceful coexistence of BASE jumpers and nature lovers took a severe hit yesterday when disagreements over the use of Mount Orion resurfaced.
"BASE jumpers are not just antisocial, but they are totally irresponsible as well," claimed Ben Blackwood, the spokesperson for Nature Watch, a local environmental organization. "The transformation of this beautiful spot into a BASE jumping mecca is not only damaging, but it is also dangerous, as the recent recovery of a wingsuit flyer by the rescue squad has shown," he continued.
Marlen Foucard, an internationally famous BASE jumper disagrees: "BASE jumping is statistically one of the safest sports there is. Accidents are not impossible, but they are unlikely. And we always work in co-operation with the local rescue teams if there are any problems."

	Original word	Prefix	Suffix	New word form	Meaning
unacceptable	accept (v)	un-	-able	adj	inakzeptabel, unzumutbar
coexistence					
disagreement					
resurface					
antisocial					
irresponsible					
environmental					
organization					
transformation					
damaging					
dangerous					
recovery					
internationally					
disagreement					
statistically					
impossible					
unlikely					
co-operation					

3 My image, my style

WORKING WITH WORDS

1 BODY IMAGE: VERBS

>> SB, S21

Complete the text with the most suitable verbs from the list. Make any changes that are necessary.

acknowledge • celebrate • encourage • glamorize • inspire • promote • relate • shame

Jameela Jamil ______________________ [1] people to post positive messages online about their bodies. Her campaign 'I Weigh' was ______________________ [2] by posts showing how little famous media personalities weighed. She is trying to make celebrities ______________________ [3] the influence they have over how young women in particular ______________________ [4] to their own bodies. Jamil, who herself has been ______________________ [5] online for her own body weight, wants people to ______________________ [6] their achievements instead of their weight. According to Jamil, influencers are ______________________ [7] being anorexic and ______________________ [8] completely unrealistic lifestyles.

2 BODY IMAGE: COLLOCATIONS

>> SB, S22–23

Complete the phrases and collocations with suitable words from pages 22–23 of the SB.

1 Jamil Jameela is a role ______________ for lots of teenage girls who worry about their body image.
2 Marvin is great fun to be with: he has a wonderful sense of ______________.
3 Body ______________ means accepting your body as it is, no matter what shape or size it is.
4 Cosmetic ______________ is one way of changing your appearance.
5 It is still rare to see plus-______________ models at fashion shows.
6 Self-______________ people worry about how other people see them.
7 If you have low self-______________, you are not confident about your character, your abilities or appearance.
8 Fashion magazines are full of airbrushed ______________ of perfect bodies.
9 Mikey is a tattoo ______________ and he has his own tattoo studio although he is only 21.

3 WORD FORMATION

>> SB, S24–25

Complete the table with the correct form of the given words. Only use your dictionary for help if you need to.

Verb	Noun (person / thing)	Noun (abstract)
to employ		
		labour
to manufacture		
		consumption / consumerism
		management
to contribute		

GRAMMAR

1 SOME, ANY, MUCH, MANY, A LOT OF

» SB, S23

Circle the correct word/phrase to complete the sentences.

1 Rishi has got any / some tattoos but he hasn't got any / some piercings.
2 How many / much tattoos has he got altogether?
3 Is there anywhere / somewhere on his body that isn't covered in tattoos?
4 He doesn't have a lot of / some tattoos on his chest, but there are a lot / any on his arms.
5 How many / much money has he spent on tattoos? – A lot / Much!
6 Rishi has any / some plans for new tattoos. He always has a lot of / many good ideas.

2 FEW, LITTLE, LOT(S), MUCH

» SB, S23

Choose the correct word or phrase from the list to replace the German word in brackets.

(a) few • (a) little • a lot of / lots of • much

1 Jameela Jamil got ______________ (viele) new followers with her 'I Weigh' campaign.
2 She has ______________ (wenig) time for people who glamorize unrealistic body images.
3 ______________ (ein paar) people have criticized her, but she has had ______________ (viel) support.
4 She thinks it will take ______________ (etwas) time before celebrities understand how ______________ (viel) influence they have.
5 Very ______________ (wenige) people think that celebrity posts are just harmless fun.
6 Is there ______________ (eine große) chance that social media will change in the next ______________ (paar) years?

3 UNCOUNTABLE NOUNS

» SB, S25; GF22, S272

Circle the correct word / phrase to complete the newspaper article.

There was / were [1] some good news from the world of fashion today: a number of leading charities have started a campaign to reduce the amount of garbage / garbages [2] that the fashion industry produces. 430,000 tons of clothes are thrown away in the UK and the rubbish is / rubbishes are [3] sent to landfills. The charities are offering advice / advices [4] and information / informations [5] on where items of clothing can be swapped or recycled. They hope that consumers will change their behaviour / behaviours [6] and treat clothes with more respect. The politics, however, is / are [7] much more difficult. Economics is / are [8] still the top priority for fashion companies as they are keen to sell as much as possible. However, recent research shows / researches show [9] that clothing manufacturing causes huge damage / damages [10] to the environment and that it is time to make progress / progresses [11] on environmental waste / wastes [12].

Tip

Your **clothes** *(pl)* are the things that you wear, such as shirts, jeans, dresses or jumpers.
Clothing is more formal than **clothes** and often means 'a particular type of clothes', e.g. *ladies clothing*.

BUILDING SKILLS

>> SB, S20; SF4, S238–239

READING FOR GIST

Is fast fashion going out of fashion?

(1) Why is it that our wardrobes are crammed with clothes even though we only wear a small percentage of them regularly? And everyone has items of clothing tucked away at the back that they have never worn at all. Just seemed like a good idea at the time! So what to do when there is no more room on your shelves. Throw something away to make to make more space. However, there is a different way ...

(2) The growing popularity of clothes sharing and swapping platforms is challenging our current throwaway culture and is providing a sustainable alternative to fast fashion. They are not only a cheap and exciting way to get your hands on new items of clothing, but they also offer a genuine alternative to textile waste and pollution. People around the world are being encouraged to stop buying new clothes and reduce their contribution to excessive fashion manufacture. If you use a swapping or sharing platform, you will never get bored with your wardrobe. And how many people can say that?

(3) Swapping platforms throw the whole idea of 'owning' clothes into question, which is no bad thing as the number of fashion seasons has increased from two a year to as many as 50–100 micro seasons per year. The fashion industry is constantly aiming to produce a new 'look'. According to the EU, the average amount of clothing bought has increased by 40% over the last 10 years. We buy more than we need and 85% of our clothes end up in landfills.

(4) There are all kinds of clothes sharing apps and platforms available: some allow you to either sell or rent out second-hand clothes; some organize regular clothes 'exchanges' throughout the year; others concentrate on children's clothing only because they grow fast and need a wardrobe that keeps up with their growth; some offer to recycle your old clothes. However, they all offer a framework for clothes sharing and encourage their users to reduce the environmental damage caused by the fashion industry. (348 words)

A Read the heading and introduction to the magazine article above. What do the following words and phrases mean?

1 fast fashion ______

2 to go out of fashion ______

3 clothes sharing platform ______

4 to challenge sth ______

5 throwaway culture ______

B Now skim the paragraphs (1–4) and match them to the topics (a–e) below. There is one more topic than you need.

a contribution of clothes swapping platforms to the environment ______

b damage done by fast fashion industry ______

c different types of clothes swapping platforms ______

d the things you need to do to get your clothes ready for swapping ______

e the situation in most people's wardrobes ______

C What is the author's aim in writing this text? Choose the most suitable summary.

a to highlight recent developments in the fast fashion industry

b to inform readers about new swapping platforms and apps

c to make fun of people with unused clothes in their wardrobe

d to point out all the ways that fast fashion harms the environment

4 Stress and pressure

WORKING WITH WORDS

1 WORD FIELD: SUNEUNG

>> SB, S26–27

Complete the text with the most suitable words from the list.

burden • degree • extracurricular • income • isolation • pressure • prestigious • prospects • ranking • revision • school leavers • tutors • well-being

For students in South Korea, the Suneung exam is the high point of all the ____________[1] put on them throughout their years at school. ____________[2] take the Suneung exam in the hope of being accepted by a ____________[3] university. Acceptance means that their job ____________[4] and probable ____________[5] increase dramatically. The best jobs go to students with a ____________[6] from one of the best universities. Learning for the Suneung exam puts a huge ____________[7] of expectation on young people and leaves them with no time for friends or for ____________[8] activities. The result is that many teenagers suffer from ____________[9] while not enough is done for their ____________[10]. The many hours of ____________[11], often under the watchful eye of private ____________[12], is also a huge expense for parents, who want their children to be at the top of the national ____________[13].

2 WORD FORMATION

>> SB, S31–32

Complete the table with the missing nouns.

Verb	Noun	Verb	Noun
to abuse		to judge	
to cure		to press	
to enforce		to recover	
to guide		to surrender	
to influence		to treat	

3 PHRASAL VERBS

>> SB, S31

Match the phrasal verbs 1–8 with the correct meaning a–h.

1 break *down*
2 come *across* sb
3 drop *out* of sth
4 give *in* to sth
5 go *on* to do sth
6 run *out* of sth
7 turn *into* sth
8 turn *to* sb

a to leave school/college without finishing
b to move to the next thing
c to become sth different
d to use up or finish sth
e to fail, to come to an end
f to (agree to) do something you don't want to do
g to go to sth/sb for help
h to meet sb by chance

1 __ 2 __ 3 __ 4 __ 5 __ 6 __ 7 __ 8 __

GRAMMAR

1 ADJECTIVES AND ADVERBS

» SB, S29–30; GF17, S268

Circle the correct word to complete the sentences.

1 In South Korea, the Suneung exam is so important / importantly because it can serious / seriously affect young people's job prospects.

2 Even organized / organizedly students who revise diligent / diligently feel nervous / nervously when they think about the results of the exam.

3 Usual / Usually, students have private / privately tuition in the evenings during the week, and at weekends they normal / normally go to revising rooms.

4 They have to do good / well in the exam to get a place at a prestigious / prestigiously university, but the competition among students is tough / toughly.

5 Even though they work hard / hardly, all students have an anxious / anxiously wait before the results are published.

6 Many students get depressed / depressedly and are scared / scaredly to tell their parents their results.

2 COMPARING ADJECTIVES AND ADVERBS

» SB, S29–30; GF18, S269

Complete the sentences with the correct form of the word at the end of the sentences. The symbols in brackets tell you which form you should use.

+ *-er / more ... than* ++ *-est / the most* = *as ... as* ≠ *not as ... as*

Haru	**Seok**	**Yuri**	**Jin**

1 Haru works *harder than* (+) Seok, but *not as hard as* (≠) Yuri. Jin works *the hardest* (++) of them all. (hard)

2 Haru's score was ________ (+) than Seok's but ________ (≠) Jin's. Yuri had ________ (++) score of them all. (low)

3 Jin's hogwan is ________ (≠) Seok's but it is ________ (+) than Haru's. Yuri's hogwan is ________ (++). (cheap)

4 Yuri's hogwan has ________ (++) exam pass rate, as it is ________ (+) than Jin's. The exam pass rate for Haru's hogwan is ________ (=) Jin's but it is ________ (≠) Yuri's. (high)

5 Seok explains things to his friends just ________ (=) Jin, but Haru explains things even ________ (+) Seok. Yuri explains things ________ (++) of them all. (good)

6 The conditions in Seok's hogwan are ________ (+) than in Jin's, but ________ (≠) in Haru's. The conditions in Yuri's hogwan are ________ (++) of them all. (bad)

7 Jin reads ________ (+) Yuri, but ________ (≠) Seok does. Haru reads ________ (++) of them all. (thorough)

BUILDING SKILLS

» SB, S30–31; SF9, S248

ANALYSING STATISTICS

A Label diagrams A–C with the correct term: bar chart, line graph or pie chart.

Drug-related crime (Jan)

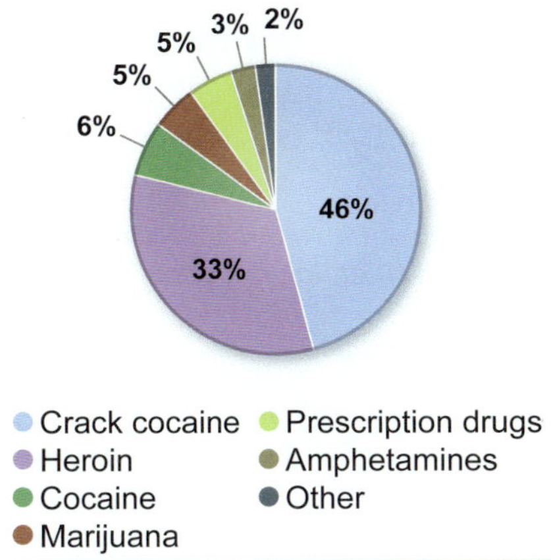

A ______________________

Drug-related crime (Jan–Jun)

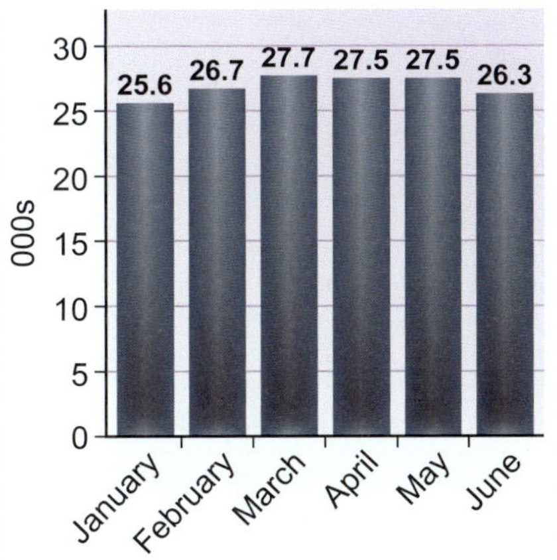

B ______________________

Drug sales (2020–2025)

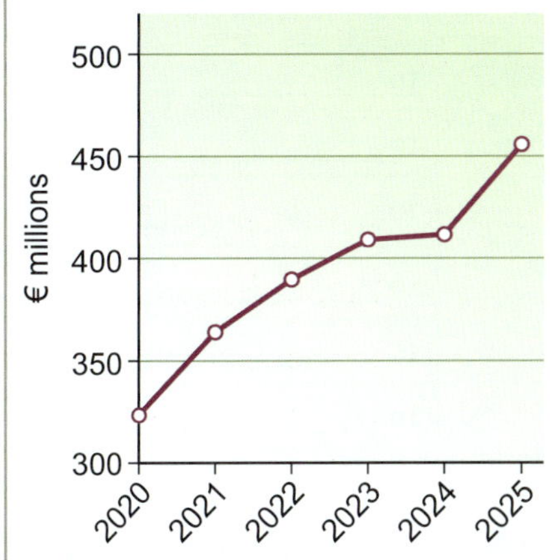

C ______________________

B Which diagrams show the following information? Tick the correct boxes. More than one answer may be correct.

1	information in numbers	A ☐	B ☐	C ☐
2	information in euros	A ☐	B ☐	C ☐
3	information as a percentage	A ☐	B ☐	C ☐
4	information for one month only	A ☐	B ☐	C ☐
5	information for a number of months	A ☐	B ☐	C ☐
6	information for a number of years	A ☐	B ☐	C ☐
7	information for all types of drugs	A ☐	B ☐	C ☐
8	information for different types of drugs	A ☐	B ☐	C ☐

C Use the words from task A and the phrases below to describe the information in each chart.

subject	types of figure	period of time
• the amount of drug sales • the total drug-related crimes • the different type of drug-related crimes	• in thousands • in millions of euros • as a percentage of the total	• for the month(s) of • January • for the years • 2020 to 2025 • January to June

1 The *pie chart* shows ____.

2 The __________ shows ____.

3 This __________ shows ____.

D Write an analysis of the three charts in your exercise book.

5 My working life

WORKING WITH WORDS

1 COLLOCATIONS WITH 'JOB'

>> SB, S49

Complete the table with the missing words.

to ______________	your	job	*gekündigt werden*
to ______________	a		*sich um eine Stelle bewerben*
to ______________	a ______________		*Teilzeit arbeiten*
to ______________ sb	a		*jemandem einen Job anbieten*
to ______________	your		*Ihren Job kündigen*
to ______________	jobs		*Arbeitsplätze schaffen*

2 NOUN COLLOCATIONS

>> SB, S48–49+54

Complete the sentences with the missing words from the list.

benefits • canteen • car • conditions • contributions • holiday • insurance • leave • pay • prospects • satisfaction • security (2×) • shift

1 Job ______________ is one of the main requirements for young people when deciding on a career. As they are more likely to change jobs than their parents, job ______________ is not considered so important.

2 Working ______________ are also important, including working hours and ______________ work.

3 For people who are not self-employed, health ______________, sick ______________, pension ______________ and social ______________ are all taken for granted in Germany.

4 For those people working freelance or in the gig economy, these benefits are not included, along with paid ______________ or an annual ______________.

5 Some of the most popular job ______________ are a subsidized ______________ and a company ______________.

6 Career or promotion ______________ also play an important role.

3 WORD FORMATION

>> SB, S58–59

Complete the gaps with the correct form of the word in brackets.

The rapid ______________ [1] (expand) of the gig economy is considered to be a modern form of worker ______________ [2] (exploit) by trade union experts. Workers are attracted by the idea of working as an ______________ [3] (independence) contractor and the ______________ [4] (flexibility) working hours that this offers. However, this working model in fact offers the workers very little legal ______________ [5] (protect) and makes them ______________ [6] (liability) for many of the costs that employers normally pay for their employees. Despite this, gig economy workers are in ______________ [7] (abundance) supply and the high levels of ______________ [8] (compete) among them only add to their ______________ [9] (insecure).

GRAMMAR

1 THE FUTURE: SIMPLE PRESENT AND PRESENT PROGRESSIVE

» SB, S52; GF9, S261

Circle the correct verb form (simple present or present progressive) to complete the dialogue. Which one sentence doesn't refer to the future?

A Do you come / Are you coming to my party tomorrow evening?

B I hope so. But tomorrow is / is being my first day at my internship with Smith Partners.

A They're in London, aren't they? How do you get / are you getting there tomorrow morning?

B My Mum takes / is taking me to the station to make sure I get the train on time. It leaves / is leaving at 7.15.

A Cool! So will you make it to my party?

B My train arrives / is arriving at 6.45 and Dad picks / is picking me up from the station. So I should have enough to get to your party.

2 THE FUTURE: *WILL*-FUTURE AND *GOING TO*-FUTURE

» SB, S55; GF9, S261

Complete the sentences with the most suitable form (*will*-future or *going to*-future) of the verbs in brackets.

Hi Brian

I've got some interesting news for you. I ________________ [1] (start) a new job in PR next month. And the best thing about it is that I ________________ [2] (leave) this boring company at last! The new job ________________ [3] (be) a big challenge, I know, but I think it ________________ [4] (give) me a chance to get more experience working with people. And on top of that, the company ________________ [5] (pay) for me to do a special training course in online marketing ... and I'm sure it ________________ [6] (be) great fun. But don't worry. I ________________ [7] (not work) all the time ... I ________________ [8] (still/have) time to meet up with my friends (I hope!). I ________________ [9] (be) in town at the weekend. ________________ [10] (you/have) time to meet for a drink?

All the best, Jenny

3 THE FUTURE: MIXED TENSES

» SB, S52+55; GF9, S261

A Choose the most suitable form (simple present, present progressive, *will*-future or *going to*-future) of the verbs in brackets. Sometimes more than one answer is possible.

Leon ________________ [1] (start) a new job next week which he thinks ________________ [2] (give) him more independence and flexibility. He ________________ [3] (deliver) for a courier company. His shifts ________________ [4] (start) at 7 a.m. but they ________________ [5] (not finish) until all his packages have been delivered. Adriana ________________ [6] (quit) her job as a taxi driver. She ________________ [7] (start) as a night security guard in an office complex next month. Her shift ________________ [8] (begin) at 7 p.m. and ________________ [9] (finish) at 7 a.m., but she hopes the new job ________________ [10] (give) her more job security.

B Write a short paragraph in your exercise book about a new job, using all four forms of the future.

SKILLS: READING

>> SB, SF4, S238

1 UNDERSTANDING THE TEXT

>> SB, SF4, S238

A Read the heading and introduction of the text on page 19, then skim the text quickly. What is the main message of the text? Tick the correct box.

a microworking is a good job to earn some extra cash ☐

b microworking is a lonely and boring job ☐

c microworking is a very badly paid job ☐

B Now scan the first six paragraphs of the text (lines 3–18) to find the following information.

1 estimated hourly wage for microworkers ______

2 number of people interviewed for the survey ______

3 percentage of microworkers earning less than the minimum wage ______

4 percentage of microworkers doing unpaid work per hour ______

5 countries with lots of microworkers ______

2 READING FOR DETAIL

A Now read the first six paragraphs of the text (lines 3–18) in detail to find the following information.

1 the types of activity involved in microworking:

- ______
- ______
- ______

2 reasons why microworking is increasing in the UK:

- ______
- ______

3 reasons why pay for microworkers is so low:

- ______
- ______

B Now read paragraphs 7 and 8 (lines 19–27) and match them to the aspects in the list (a–f). There are two aspects per paragraph.

a working conditions

b idea of non-stop work

c influence of social media

d microworkers in developing countries

e new technological developments

f political demands

paragraph 7 (lines 19–23) ____ ____
paragraph 8 (lines 24–27) ____ ____

C Now read the last two paragraphs of the text (lines 28–34) and note down four disadvantages microworkers face.

- ______
- ______
- ______
- ______

Britain's hidden online 'microworkers' paid less than £4 an hour

Call to name and shame firms paying below the minimum wage for gig economy tasks like data entry

Workers engaging in a rapidly growing form of unregulated internet labour known as microwork are routinely being denied the minimum wage, it can be revealed.

An investigation by the thinktank Autonomy and researchers at the University of Exeter and the London School of Economics suggests that thousands could be earning less than £4 an hour.

Microworkers perform simple tasks such as identifying and captioning images to nudge along artificial intelligence operations, data entry, or simply clicking on ads to drive traffic. The industry grew during the pandemic as people were forced to work from home.

But the survey of 1,189 UK-based microworkers suggests that, like others in the gig economy who are not classified as employees under employment law, wages are often below the minimum wage.

Almost two in three said they earn less than £4 an hour under piece-wage terms in which they are paid per task, with 95% making less than the UK minimum wage. The hourly rate is effectively even worse as workers must spend time securing new assignments. Some 30% of microworkers said they spend at least half an hour on unpaid activities per hour of paid work.

Most microworkers, who number well into the millions, are from countries such as India, Kenya and Venezuela but with wages flatlining in the UK amid a cost of living crisis even such low wages are becoming increasingly attractive for Britons.

The report said: 'Microwork and other forms of digital piece work are beginning to play an important role within neoliberal "hustle culture": the idea that individuals ought to be productive all of the time and that success is determined by endless work and the attainment of an entrepreneurial ideal. Due to the influence of a pervasive "always on" culture promoted by celebrities and influencers on social media, many workers feel guilty when not working.'

Will Stronge, director of research at Autonomy, said the UK government should 'name and shame the companies paying microworkers below the minimum wage' and 'unfairly exploiting thousands of microworkers' in an 'exploding industry which has zero regulation'. He added: 'This invisible online workforce deserves better compensation and protections in work.'

Microworkers often have no relationship with the people they work for. One microworker from the east of England told the *Observer*: 'It's difficult to get in touch with anyone from these platforms to say if there's an issue or the system is not functioning. It's faceless, you're part of a machine. Things are quite one-sided.'

He began doing microwork during the pandemic, and he welcomes the fact that he can work during the hours once spent commuting. But 'the pay is low when you put it into context and I think the companies and platforms are getting some very cheap labour out of it,' he added. 'You might also get your work rejected and that means you don't get paid for it. If I was relying on this for my main income, I would be very concerned.'

(511 words)

From: The Guardian, 25 June 2022

SKILLS: WRITING

>> SB, SF6, S242

Discuss the following statement:

'Working to live is better than living to work. Everyone can achieve that goal.'

1 UNDERSTANDING THE TASK

A Read the task above and tick what you have to do:

- a convince the reader that your opinion on the statement is correct ☐
- b examine both sides of the argument and then state which you agree with ☐
- c examine both sides of the argument without stating your opinion ☐

B Which of the following should be the main aspect you need to discuss?

- a in-company working conditions ☐
- b microworking ☐
- c modern working methods ☐
- d balance between work and social life ☐
- e the gender pay gap ☐
- f the gig economy ☐

2 COLLECTING IDEAS

A Read the text 'How young people are reinventing the office' on page 56 of the SB and add ideas to the headings below.

work-life balance

- flexible working hours ______________________________
- salary/paycheck ______________________________
- burnout ______________________________
- career/promotion prospects ______________________________
- employers ______________________________
- white-collar workers ______________________________
- remote working ______________________________
- own ideas ______________________________

B Highlight the arguments in your mind map that support the statement in one colour; highlight arguments against it in a different colour.

3 STRUCTURING YOUR IDEAS

A Choose the two strongest arguments for and against the given statement. Write down the stronger argument first. Add any supporting statements or examples that you can think of.

Arguments for:		*examples / supporting statements:*
1		
2		
Arguments against:		*examples / supporting statements:*
1		
2		

B Now decide which side of the argument you agree with and note down your opinion and your reasons.

4 INTRODUCING THE DISCUSSION

The introduction to an essay should do the things listed below. Read the introductions (a–d) and tick the aspects each one achieves. Which one would you use to introduce your discussion?

An introduction should ...	a	b	c	d
• refer to the topic/question/statement of the essay	☐	☐	☐	☐
• explain what the essay is going to do	☐	☐	☐	☐
• use impersonal, neutral language	☐	☐	☐	☐
• be short and concise	☐	☐	☐	☐

a	Everybody knows that working too hard is bad for you. In this essay I'm going to look at work-life balance.
b	Many people think that too much work is unhealthy. In this essay I'm going to examine the pros and cons of a good work-life balance.
c	A healthy work-life balance is a major priority for many young people when choosing their career. This essay will discuss the advantages and disadvantages of a balanced work and social life and consider whether it is possible for everyone to achieve.
d	In this essay I will first of all list and analyse the potential benefits of a healthy work-life balance, then show you some of the possible drawbacks to trying to achieve this balance. Finally, I will discuss the question of whether it is possible for everyone to achieve a good work-life balance.

5 WRITING THE DISCUSSION

Now write your discussion in your exercise book, using your notes from exercise 3. Include an introduction and conclusion.

6 Connected worlds

WORKING WITH WORDS

1 COLLOCATIONS AND COMPOUNDS

» SB, S66–67

Join each word or phrase from A with one from B. They can all be found in the text 'The Changing Face of News Media'

A appeal to • echo • engage with • free • get • go • mobile • multi- • on the • open- • reading • reinforce

B access to • chamber • device • go • minded • of charge • preferences • someone's conscience • someone's views • someone's views • tasking • viral

2 SOCIAL MEDIA ADJECTIVES

» SB, S70–71

A Find 12 adjectives to describe the tone of social media posts.

S	P	R	O	M	A	N	T	I	C	E
A	R	T	I	F	I	C	I	A	L	X
S	E	S	N	A	R	K	Y	U	A	U
H	T	F	H	O	N	E	S	T	U	B
I	E	A	S	O	C	A	L	H	G	E
N	N	K	U	F	L	A	S	E	H	R
G	T	E	G	U	S	H	I	N	G	A
A	I	N	T	E	R	E	S	T	R	N
H	O	S	T	I	L	E	N	I	E	T
A	U	W	H	I	M	S	I	C	A	L
T	**S**	**I**	**N**	**C**	**E**	**R**	**E**	I	N	G

1 aufrichtig *sincere*
2 ausgelassen ______
3 böse ______
4 echt ______
5 ehrlich ______
6 feindselig ______
7 hochgestochen ______
8 künstlich ______
9 romantisch ______
10 skurril, launenhaft ______
11 überschwänglich ______
12 unecht ______

B Think about your recent social media posts. Use five of the adjectives to describe them. Be honest!

3 CORRECT WORD

» SB, S74–77

Cross out the two of the four words in italics which do not fit in the sentence.

1 A successful influencer has to be a skilled *brand ambassador* • ~~*celebrity*~~ • ~~*follower*~~ • *storyteller.*
2 Influencers use social media to reach out to their *audience* • *brands* • *clients* • *followers.*
3 Every influencer needs to develop a clear *content* • *niche* • *schedule* • *specialization.*
4 It is part of the influencer's role to *develop* • *filter* • *promote* • *review* products.
5 Influencers have to work hard to gain followers' *credibility* • *integrity* • *respect* • *trust.*
6 It is important for influencers to *communicate* • *hold* • *meet* • *respect* deadlines.
7 An influencer's work must adhere to *advertisements* • *consumers* • *expectations* • *guidelines.*
8 Influencers are *following* • *promoting* • *running* • *sponsoring* their own business.
9 Companies may choose to *advertise* • *endorse* • *promote* • *sponsor* their products themselves.

GRAMMAR

1 THE PASSIVE: SPOTTING AND CORRECTING ERRORS

>> SB, S68; GF13, S265

The writer of the text below has made some mistakes using passive forms. Find eight passive sentences and correct them.

In recent decades, our news has changed completely by new technology. In the 'old days', newspaper publishers printed written news about recent events. Live news were produced by broadcasting corporations. The distinction was obvious and well understood. Nowadays, articles, videos and podcasts are often publish by the same organization on the same website.

The distinction between fact and opinion is being losed with the change to an informal and user-friendly presentation style. The news has being made 'sexier' to grab our attention. 'Clickbait' is often use to arouse our curiousity. Juicy gossip are promised by headlines which then aren't discussed in the actual story.

News has become a 24-hour business, requiring frequent updates and ever more material. Stories circulate rapidly around the globe. Fake news are sometimes reported even by respected news sources. (134 words)

2 THE PASSIVE: COMPLETING SENTENCES

>> SB, S68; GF13, S265

Complete the sentences with suitable passive forms of the verbs in brackets.

1 Do you think that the recent election *was affected* by fake news? (affect)
2 A lot of our news ____________ 'on the go' these days. (read)
3 The news in our feed ____________ by an algorithm which predicts our interests. (choose)
4 I would have read the article, but I ____________ by the paywall. (stop)
5 I uploaded the photo yesterday and within hours it ____________ around the world. (share)
6 Tailored messaging ____________ even more in the future. (use)
7 It is important for the public to ____________ to different perspectives. (expose)
8 I do not trust this story: it ____________ independently. (not – verify)
9 News reporting ____________ by the introduction of new technology in the 1990s. (transform)
10 Who knows what new communication methods ____________ in the decades to come? (introduce)
11 Perhaps our ability to check facts ____________ by new developments in Artificial Intelligence. (soon – improve)
12 Since the invention of the internet, more information ____________ available to us than ever before. (make)

SKILLS: LISTENING

>> SB, SF5, S240

1 PREPARING TO LISTEN: UNDERSTANDING THE GIST

>> SB, S70–73

Match headings a–f with quotations 1–6.

a uncaring, attention-seeking behaviour ____
b too much negativity online ____
c uncritical attitudes of influencers and fans ____
d spreading kindness for altruistic motives ____
e invasion of personal privacy ____
f more to the story than appears at first sight ____

1 'I was just minding my own business. The last thing I wanted was to appear in a YouTube video.'
2 'However, if we look a little more closely, these apparently kind actions are not always well received.'
3 'I think he was just showing off his generosity – at my expense.'
4 'My hope is to inspire others through my videos on social media, so that they get out there and make the world a better place.'
5 'There's so much hate and anger in the internet. Why do we behave so badly online?'
6 'As social media users, shouldn't we be media-savvy enough to recognize when our emotions are being manipulated?'

2 MULTIPLE MATCHING

2

You are going to hear four people talking about 'random acts of kindness' on social media.

While listening, match the headings a to f with the speakers 1 to 4. There are two more headings than you need.

Tip
In this type of task, you must listen for gist – the main ideas expressed in the recording. Your answers to task 1 will help you.

a uncaring, attention-seeking behaviour
b too much negativity online
c uncritical attitudes of influencers and fans
d spreading kindness for altruistic motives
e invasion of personal privacy
f more to the story than appears at first sight

Speaker	1	2	3	4
Heading				

Headings not used: ____ ____

3 PREPARING TO LISTEN

>> SB, S74–77

Complete each statement with just a few words, using information from the quotation.

1 Advertisements follow users who show interest in the product but ______________________

'If you look at a product online but don't buy it the first time, they can "remind" you to complete the transaction. The idea is that the ad targets people who have shown an interest in a product, instead of advertising to random web users.'

2 Cookies pass on our information to ______________________

'Cookies enable a site to track our browsing habits, see what we're looking at ... and then they follow us to another site and communicate that information to that site, so that it can serve up suitable ads.'

3 Political groups may want to ______________________

'If political organizations know a lot about us, they can manipulate our voting behaviour in specific ways. For example, they can persuade indecisive voters that it's not worth going out to vote at all.'

4 To avoid being tracked you ______________________ your online behaviour.

'If you're determined to do something, you can change your browser settings to reject tracking cookies. Maybe you should avoid services like popular search engines altogether. Use a virtual private network to browse the internet anonymously. Stop using social media.'

4 QUESTIONS ON THE TEXT

3

The speaker talks about her experience with tracking advertisements. Listen to the audio file and answer the questions in English based on the information you hear.

Tip
In this type of task, you must listen for specific details. Your answers to task 3 will help you.

1 Why do the same advertisements follow us around online?

____

2 Why do different people see different advertisements on the same site?

____

3 How do we give advertisers a lot of useful data? *(three activities)*

____

____

4 What can political parties do with our data?

____

5 Why is the narrator concerned about giving information to her country's government?

____

6 How can we prevent the harvesting of our data? *(four aspects)*

____

____

____

7 What is the alternative to changing our internet use?

____

SKILLS: MEDIATION (ENGLISH–GERMAN)

>>SB, SF10, S250

1 DIE AUFGABE ANALYSIEREN

>>SB, S70–73

Lesen Sie die Mediationsaufgabe unten und vervollständigen Sie die Analyse dazu.

SITUATION: Ein Internetfreund hat sich vorgenommen, in Zukunft weniger Zeit auf Social Media-Seiten zu verbringen, da er über die „Filterblasen-Theorie" gelesen hat und nicht möchte, dass sein Weltbild verzerrt wird. Sie finden seine Ängste übertrieben und möchten ihn vom Gegenteil überzeugen.

AUFGABE: Sie lesen den Artikel „Bursting the Bubble" auf S. 27, Anschließend schreiben Sie Ihrem Internetfreund eine E-Mail, in der Sie auf folgende Punkte eingehen:

- wie sich Menschen offline Informationen beschaffen
- wie sich Menschen online Informationen beschaffen
- wer für die eigenen Informationsquellen letztendlich verantwortlich ist

Analyse der Mediationsaufgabe

Ursprungstext: *Bursting the Bubble*

Adressat: ____________________

Medium/Textsorte: ____________________

Zweck: ____________________

Sprachebene: ____________________

2 DEN INHALT ANALYSIEREN

A Lesen Sie den Text auf Seite 27 und notieren Sie die Absätze, welche die folgenden Themen behandeln.

a Typischer Nachrichtenkonsum: Offline-Medien ____________________

b Typischer Nachrichtenkonsum: Online-Medien ____________________

c Nachrichtenvolumen offline vs. online ____________________

d Austauschmöglichkeiten offline vs. online ____________________

e Wie man eine aufgeschlossene Weltanschauung pflegen kann ____________________

B Notieren Sie die Absätze, die für Ihre Mediationstext irrelevant sind.

____

C Lesen Sie den Text gründlich durch und schreiben Sie Stichwörter zu den folgenden Punkten auf.

a wie sich Menschen offline Informationen beschaffen

____

____

b wie wir uns online Informationen beschaffen

____

____

c wer für die eigenen Informationsquellen letztendlich verantwortlich ist

____

____

3 VERFASSEN DER MEDIATION

Schreiben Sie nun Ihren Mediationstext in Ihr Heft.

Bursting the Bubble

[1] The theory of social media 'bubbles', how they work and how they distort our view of reality, is well known. It has been written about by authors such as internet activist and entrepreneur Eli Pariser, who invented the term 'filter bubble'.

[2] In his 2011 book *The Filter Bubble*, Pariser argues that internet companies limit our access to information rather than expanding it. It supposedly works like this:

[3] Social media algorithms feed us more of what we have indicated that we like, e.g. through clicks, reactions, search histories and friend lists. As a result, we can easily find ourselves in a state of isolation, where we are rarely confronted with good arguments against our beliefs and opinions. In other words, we may find ourselves in a 'filter bubble': everything we disagree with has been filtered out.

[4] In Pariser's view, this effect is not an unfortunate accidental consequence of social media. It is deliberate and designed into the system. It is part of the business strategy of giant corporations such as Google, Meta, Microsoft and Apple which control our access to the internet – a strategy which aims to exploit our data and manipulate our views.

[5] However, it is far from clear that this filter effect is something new or specific to the online world. When people are offline, they tend to use the same few trusted news sources all the time. This seems to be how we have always found out about the world around us. Our parents and grandparents always read the same newspaper, watch the same TV news bulletin. Hardly anyone except journalists or academics regularly buys a pile of different newspapers and compares them.

[6] In other words, we have always selected our own information sources to fit in with our pre-existing views and values – and offline most of us are *more* selective.

[7] This is where the 'filter bubble' theory may really fall apart.

[8] Online, we are more likely to get served up *news that we did not choose*. Our online news comes from more sources and is more diverse. There is less opportunity to practise loyalty to one or two sources. According to research by Reuters Institute and the University of Oxford, more than two thirds of the news we see online is incidental – it is part of our social media news feed, comes via mobile alerts, or pops up in search results.

[9] Another point to bear in mind is that people who use social media are exposed to *more* news, in terms of sheer quantity of words and images, than people who do not use it.

[10] Furthermore, thanks to social media we have opportunities for discussion with people all over the world. These opportunities barely exist offline.

[11] Whether or not filter bubbles exist, and whether or not they are a problem: we individual internet users are the ones in ultimate control of our news feeds. We can seek out different perspectives and create opportunities for respectful discussion with people who are not like us.

SKILLS: ANALYSING A CARTOON

>> SB, SF8, S246

1 ANALYSING THE TASK

>> SB, S74–77

Read the task carefully. Which of the following are you asked to do?

- a describe the cartoon ☐
- b analyse the meaning of the cartoon ☐
- c give your opinion ☐
- d compare the cartoon to your own experience ☐

Task

Describe and analyse the cartoon. Give your opinion of it.

"I want to make my mark on the world—and have it disappear in ten seconds."

CartoonStock.com

2 DESCRIBING THE CARTOON

A Describe the situation in the cartoon.

____

____

B Describe the people and their expressions in the cartoon.

____

____

C Describe the objects in the cartoon, and explain what they say about the people.

____

____

D Is there text in the cartoon? What form does it take? What does it tell us?

caption • speech bubble • thought bubble • title

____

____

3 ANALYSING THE CARTOON

A Give the general topic of the cartoon.

This cartoon examines ______________________

B Assess the attitude of the cartoonist towards the topic.

____

____

Useful expressions

calls sth into question • cruelly satirizes sth • gently sends sth up • make fun of sb/sth • takes a critical look at sth

C State the message of the cartoon.

The cartoon's message is that ______________________

4 GIVING YOUR OPINION

A Assess whether the cartoon makes his/her point successfully. Justify your assessment.

Useful expressions

caricatures • (un)convincing • cruel • exaggerate • fleeting nature • (un)funny • gentle • poke fun at • powerful • thought-provoking • use lazy stereotypes

____

____

B Say whether you like the cartoon or not. Would you show it to someone else? Explain your opinion.

____

____

5 WRITING THE TEXT

Look at the instructions again and write your text in your exercise book.

7 Diversity in society

WORKING WITH WORDS

1 IDIOMATIC VERB PHRASES

» SB, S82–85

Complete the sentences with the most suitable verbs from the list. Make any other changes that are necessary.

to add up • to come out • to cope with sth • to freak sb out • to get on • to get real • kick sb's ass • to spell sth out • to stand up to sb

1 Hey! You 're freaking ____________ me out ____________ (wahnsinning machen), man! Do I need to ____________ (Klartext reden) to you! Go away!

2 My grandad ____________ (älter werden) a bit now. He's 87 and very fit but sometimes he can't ____________ (bewältigen) the everyday tasks in his life.

3 A: The pressure from my family ____________ (zunehmen) ever since I ____________ (sich outen) to them that I am gay. They still can't accept it and want me to keep quiet about it.

B: Hey, just ____________ (sich behaupten) them for once and tell them ____________ (auf den Boden zurückkommen)! It's none of their business.

4 You ready to play? I'm going to ____________ (jdn in den Hintern treten) ! Let's get started!

2 WORD FAMILIES

» SB, S86–87

Complete the table with the missing words. Use your dictionary if necessary.

Verb	Adjective	Noun (abstract)
to complicate		
to confuse		
to forgive		
to apologize		

3 WORD BUILDING

» SB, S90–93

Complete the gaps with the correct form of the word in brackets.

One of the biggest barriers ____________ [1] (bar) for people with physical ____________ [2] (disable) is the lack of ____________ [3] (accept) by able-bodied people. This can make it difficult for them to enjoy full ____________ [4] (participate) in social activities, and their ____________ [5] (integrate) into society is ____________ [6] (challenge). There needs to be a lot more ____________ [7] (invest) in social projects and the current ____________ [8] (fundraise) is not nearly enough. We need to increase the ____________ [9] (visible) of disabled people in society so that they can interact and ____________ [10] (social) in their everyday life and not suffer from ____________ [11] (lonely). Our ____________ [12] (reputed) as a caring society depends on how we treat people with mental and physical ____________ [13] (impaired).

GRAMMAR

1 SIMPLE PAST AND PAST PROGRESSIVE

» SB S83; GF3–4, S259

Circle the correct verb form (simple past or past progressive) to complete the sentences.

1 Remy waited / was waiting to cross the street when somebody bumped / was bumping into her.
2 Sophie hit / was hitting the glass ceiling at work even though she did / was doing very well in her job.
3 Michael waited / was waiting to see the doctor with his daughter when another patient asked / was asking where her mother was.
4 Two women started / were starting to abuse Jarved but his manager told / was telling them to leave.
5 A security guard asked / was asking DeShona Williams for proof that she was a guest while she and her kids swam / were swimming in a hotel pool.
6 It was embarrassing because other guests watched / were watching while she argued / was arguing with the guard.

2 MODAL VERBS

» SB S89; GF10, S261

Complete the email with suitable modal verbs. Use the table on page 262 of the SB.

Hey Dara!

________________ [1] (Bitte) I ask you a personal question? Who are you closest to: your mom or your grandparents? You ________________ [2] (Empfehlung) think about that before you start worrying about money and your tennis career. Your grandparents ________________ [3] (Möglichkeit) want to do the right thing for you, but ________________ [4] (Fähigkeit) they give you all the love your mom has given you over the years? They might say you ________________ [5] (Erlaubnis) go and live with them, but you ________________ [6] (Verbot) throw away your relationship with your Mom. But living with your grand-parents ________________ [7] (freie Wahl) be the only option open to you. You ________________ [8] (Vorschrift) have your legal guardian's permission to play on the Tour before you are 18, so you ________________ [9] (Empfehlung) make sure that your mom is on your side whatever you do. You ________________ [10] (Erlaubnis) do whatever you want, as far as I'm concerned, but you ________________ [11] (Möglichkeit) regret it if you turn your back on your mom now.

3 RELATIVE CLAUSES

» SB, S93; GF20, S270

Complete the text with *who, which, that, whose* or *where*. Only use a relative pronoun where necessary.

Rajah lives in a flat ________________ [1] belongs to a charity ________________ [2] two sisters set up to support young people with learning disabilities. The young people ________________ [3] live there need some help in doing everyday tasks. The flat ________________ [4] they share is part of a project that also includes young people ________________ [5] are unemployed. The flatmates, ________________ [6] families often can't look after them, share all the household jobs ________________ [7] they have to do. It is a place ________________ [8] they can be independent, but still have the extra help ________________ [9] they need. Rajah, ________________ [10] has been there for a year, is proud of the progress ________________ [11] he has made.

SKILLS: READING

>> SB, SF4, S238

1 UNDERSTANDING THE TEXT

>> SB, S82–85

Read the heading and introduction of the text on page 33, then skim the text quickly. What is the text about? Tick the correct box.

a children who don't follow schools' dress codes ☐
b discrimination in Britain's schools on racial grounds ☐
c new guidelines for schools on dress codes ☐

2 MULTIPLE CHOICE

A Now read the first six paragraphs of the text (lines 3–27) and note down which paragraphs deal with the aspects listed below (a–c). (There are two paragraphs for each aspect.)

a hair discrimination ________ ________

b Makena Stevens ________ ________

c the Equality and Human Rights Commission ________ ________

B Read the paragraphs you marked and tick the correct answer according to the text.

1 The Equality and Human Rights Commission ...
a defines what afro hairs styles are. ☐
b enforces the 2010 Equality Act. ☐
c issues guidelines on discrimination. ☐
d writes dress codes for schools. ☐

2 Hair discrimination is ...
a a form of racial discrimination. ☐
b easy to identify. ☐
c is not included in the 2010 Equality Act. ☐
d very common in British schools. ☐

3 Makena Stevens ...
a changed schools because of hair discrimination. ☐
b doesn't believe schools will stop policing afro hair. ☐
c thinks the EHRC guidelines have come too late. ☐
d was helped by the EHRC to fight for her rights. ☐

3 MULTIPLE MATCHING

A Find the paragraphs in the text that contain statements from the following people:

a Department of Education spokesperson ________

b EHRC spokesperson ________

c Kalvin Bissaka ________

d Makena Stevens ________

e Tessa Trimble ________

B Now match the speakers (a–e) to the following statements:

Schools should …	Speaker
1 be a safe place for children of all races	______
2 should never discriminate against pupils because of their culture	______
3 make sure their dress codes do not discriminate against pupils	______
4 not police our afro hairstyles	______
5 recognize the needs of different ethnic groups	______

UK schools warned not to ban afro hairstyles

Equality watchdog issues new guidance intended to prevent hair discrimination

[1] Britain's equality watchdog is warning schools in England, Scotland and Wales not to penalise pupils for wearing their hair in natural afro styles, cornrows, braids or plaits. According to the Equality and Human Rights Commission (EHRC), some school dress codes and uniform policies may be unlawful if they ban certain hairstyles without allowing for exceptions on racial or religious grounds. It is therefore urging schools to review their existing policies and practices to ensure they comply with the 2010 Equality Act.

[2] A spokesperson for the EHRC was quoted as saying: 'It is our aim to stop schools from discriminating against pupils because of their appearance. Every child should be able to express their culture and heritage as they wish and not be forced to change their appearance in line with discriminatory school rules.'

[3] Discrimination can take a number of different forms according to the EHRC: this not only includes describing someone's hairstyle as exotic, but also banning certain hairstyles. Children who are affected often complain that their schools don't understand the origins of afro hairstyles and the care they need.

[4] The issue continues to be a problem in schools. As hair discrimination is a form of racial discrimination, it is protected by the Equality Act 2010. But unlike race, religion, or sexual orientation, hair texture is not explicitly a protected characteristic under the act, which makes forms of discrimination based on hair texture much more pervasive. This means that suspected cases of hair discrimination may be harder to prove compared with other forms.

[5] The EHRC provides support and advice on equality law and the new guidance has been welcomed by many families who have been affected by discrimination from schools. One such example was Makena Stevens who as a 14-year-old was regularly sent home from her south London school because of her afro-style hair. In 2022, she won a compensation payment in an out-of-court settlement after a three-year legal battle funded by the EHRC.

[6] 'The EHRC really helped me with my case,' said Stevens. 'I would've had to give up fighting the policy at my school without their support and funding. I can't believe what happened to me but it's great to know that these guidelines now exist. Afro hair is part of our identity but it is totally unreal that some schools still think it is OK to police it.'

[7] According to Tessa Trimble, an education lawyer, the EHRC guidance is 'a sharp reminder to school leaders that their dress codes and policies about hairstyles could be discriminatory and unlawful. I think many school governors will want to review their uniform policies immediately to make sure that no pupil is discriminated against because of their race or religion.'

[8] The development of the new guidance has been supported by the all-party parliamentary group for race equality in education. One member, Kalvin Bissaka, said: 'Across the whole UK, Black children should know that they can be proud of their identity. Race equality in education should be a priority for all schools so that they can provide a secure environment for pupils of all races.'

[9] A spokesperson for the Department of Education commented: 'It is unlawful to discriminate against pupils on the grounds of race and discrimination of this kind has no place in our schools. We regularly provide guidance to schools to ensure that school leaders are particularly sensitive to the needs of different cultures, races and religions and act reasonably in accommodating these needs.' (587 words)

SKILLS: WRITING

>> SB, SF6, S242

Taking the cartoon as a starting point, comment on the statement below in about 250 words.

Being disabled should not mean being disqualified from having access to every aspect of life
– Emma Thompson, British actor

1 UNDERSTANDING THE TASK

Read the task above and tick what you have to do:

a Analyse the cartoon and comment on its message. ☐
b Convince the reader that your opinion on the statement is correct. ☐
c Examine both sides of the argument and then state which you agree with. ☐
d Examine both sides of the argument without stating your opinion. ☐

2 COLLECTING IDEAS

Read the statements (a–g) below and decide whether they are 'for' or 'against' more accessibility Then write the statements in the table. Match the arguments 'against' to the correct counterarguments in favour of more accessibility. One statement is suitable as a conclusion.

a disability is a fact of life; can't be changed
b everybody should have the same chances/opportunities (principle of equality)
c governments need to do more to reduce physical and mental barriers to inclusion and more diversity
d prejudice can be removed by inclusive teaching / more contact / Paralympics & Special Olympics
e some cities/countries have done a lot to remove physical barriers
f some physical barriers can't be changed easily, e.g. old buildings, historic towns
g there are mental barriers and prejudice as well as physical barriers

Arguments against accessibility	Arguments for accessibility
Conclusion	

3 WRITING AN INTRODUCTION

You decide to write a comment agreeing with Emma Thompson's statement. Read the three introductions and decide whether they fulfil the conditions below. Choose the most suitable introduction for your comment.

a	Everybody knows that people with disabilities face a lot of obstacles in their daily life. However, I agree with Emma Thompson that being disabled should not mean being disqualified from having access to every aspect of life. That is what I am going to look at in this essay.
b	In the cartoon we can see a man in a wheelchair. He looks as if he wants to go to a workshop on accessibility. However, the entrance to the meeting place is up a flight of stairs so he will be unable to attend. I think the cartoonist is making the point that people with disabilities still face a lot of barriers.
c	Imagine you were disabled and couldn't go wherever you want or do whatever you want to do because a physical obstacle, such as the steps in the cartoon, is in your way. This situation is totally unfair but it is one that disabled people face everyday. So what can we do to improve accessibility for disabled people?

The introduction to the comment should ...	a	b	c
• refer to the topic of the comment	☐	☐	☐
• refer to the cartoon	☐	☐	☐
• catch the reader's attention	☐	☐	☐
• encourage the reader to continue reading	☐	☐	☐

4 WRITING A PARAGRAPH

You decide to use these arguments in the first paragraph of the main body of the text.

Argument	*disability is a fact of life; can't be changed*
Counterargument	*everybody should have the same chances/opportunities (principle of equality)*

A Choose one of the following topic statements to start your paragraph. Remember that the topic statement should say what the paragraph is about but not give your personal opinion.

a	According to the UN Declaration of Human Rights, all people are born equal, but not everybody has the same chances and opportunities because they are born with disabilities.	☐
b	Although disability is a fact of life that cannot be changed, most people agree that everybody should have the same chances and opportunities.	☐
c	Some people say that disability is a fact of life and cannot be changed, however I believe that everybody should have the same chances or opportunities.	☐

B Now complete your paragraph in your exercise book, giving reasons and examples.

C Write the next two paragraphs in your exercise book using these topic sentences. (Look at the table in task 2.)

While some things, such as historic old town centres, are difficult to adapt, some local councils have done a lot in recent years to improve access.

The biggest obstacle to inclusion is the prejudice that disabled people face from other people.

5 WRITING A CONCLUSION

Now use the remaining statement from exercise 2, or your own ideas, to conclude your comment in your exercise book.

8 Multicultural societies

WORKING WITH WORDS

1 WORD FAMILIES: REFUGEE EXPERIENCE

>> SB, S98–101

Complete the table. There may be more than one adjective form. Find as many as you can.

Verb	Adjective	Noun
	dead, deadly, dying	
endure		
		fear
persecute		
resent		
	starved, starving	
		suspicion
	tense	
		threat

2 WORD GRID: SYMBOLS AND VALUES

>> SB, S106–109

Complete the grid using the clues in the sentences.

1 ____ is one of the worst forms of economic exploitation.

2 Every human being has a right to ____.

3 Colston's work for ____ does not excuse his racism.

4 These monuments are not in keeping with the ____ of our times.

5 The ____ were all white men: we need more diversity in our art.

6 We can learn about historical figures without commemorating them with ____.

7 Public monuments ought to be a source of community ____.

8 Does destroying works of art harm our ____ of expression?

9 It is difficult to see what positive ____ this vandalism sends.

1				S		A				
2			J			T				
3	C					T				
4		S				I				
5				A		T				
6		S				U				
7			P			D				
8			F			E				
9			M			S				

3 ANTONYMS: HUMAN BEHAVIOUR

>> SB, S102–105

Complete the sentences with words from the box with opposite meanings to the underlined words. There are some words that you do not need.

accept • amusement • criticize • friendly • frown • ignore • impatient • kindly • nasty • reassuring • serious

1 Her ______________ quickly turned to annoyance as he started to make racist comments.
2 He said that he wanted to compliment her scarf but in fact his intention was to ______________ her clothing.
3 Despite her efforts to be nice, she received ______________ comments from her colleagues.
4 Members of ethnic minorities are sometimes patient simply because it is unsafe to appear ______________.
5 Although he was unable to refute her arguments, he refused to ______________ them.
6 The encounter was a little scary for Tazin but her expression was intended to be ______________.
7 Her smile turned to a ______________ when she realized what he meant by his remark.
8 The woman greeted her ______________ but spoke sternly when she realized that Tazin was Muslim.

GRAMMAR

1 FORMING IF-SENTENCES: TYPE 1

>> SB, S101; GF14, S266

Match pairs of sentences, then use them to write conditional sentences. Make as many meaningful sentences as you can.

TIP
Replace nouns with pronouns instead of repeating them.

Examples:
If locals show kindness to refugees, they will feel safer.
Refugees will feel safer if locals show kindness to them.

Helmi and his family return to Syria.
Helmi finds a job.
Helmi learns to speak English fluently.
Locals are sad to see the family go.
Locals feel fear and anger.
Locals show kindness to refugees.
Media coverage is negative towards refugees.
People become refugees.

People leave their former lives behind.
People remain in war zones.
Refugee children mix with local children.
Refugee children soon learn English.
Refugees face starvation and violence.
Refugees feel safer.
Refugees feel welcome.
Refugees repay locals' kindness.

2 SPOTTING ERRORS: IF-SENTENCES TYPE 2

>> SB, S108; GF14, S266

The writer of this text has made some mistakes using conditional forms. Find seven errors and correct them. The first one is highlighted.

In Australia many place names are of European origin. You look at a map of Australia, you find names such as Balmoral, Castlemaine and Hahndorf. For most of these places, Aboriginal names already existed. Other places commemorate 19th-century public figures who were involved in racist practices, such as Macquarie and Mackay. When more people would know the history, they would understand how offensive these names are. Furthermore, if the Aboriginal place names are widely used, people might become more aware of the indigenous language, culture and history of their area. It would be more difficult for racist attitudes to persist if all Australians will be well informed about their country. However, if everyone agreed that all controversial place names must go, where did it end? The names of the states of Queensland and Victoria both commemorate the British monarch of the period. Should they be called something else? There is no Aboriginal name for them because they did not exist before colonization.

SKILLS: LISTENING

>> SB, SF05, S240

1 PREPARING TO LISTEN: KEY WORDS

>> SB, S98–101

Read the questions in task 2 below from a multiple choice listening task. Circle or highlight the key words in each sentence.

2 MULTIPLE CHOICE

4

You are going to hear a radio phone-in in which people express different attitudes towards refugees in Australia.

TIP

In this type of task, you must listen for specific details. Your answers to task 1 will help you.

Listen and choose the correct answer for each question. There is only one correct answer.

1 Haasim wants the Australian government to ...
   a make its refugee policy stricter.
   b continue its current strict refugee policy.
   c review its current refugee policy in case changes are needed.
   d relax its current strict refugee policy because times have changed.

2 According to Haasim, ending unauthorized boat arrivals from Indonesia ...
   a improved Australia's security.
   b put refugees in greater danger.
   c was unnecessary and ineffective.
   d prevented deaths of refugees at sea.

3 Beth believes that banning refugee arrivals by boat ...
   a is impossible to do effectively.
   b does not take account of the refugees' situation.
   c must be balanced by more refugee arrivals by plane.
   d is unnecessary because most refugees arrive by plane.

4 In Beth's view, concerns about the safety of boat arrivals are ...
   a just an excuse for selfishness.
   b the result of a lack of information.
   c a result of political propaganda.
   d motivated by real worries for refugee safety.

5 In Kon's view, calling arrivals by sea 'illegal' ...
   a is a political strategy to win votes.
   b is a misunderstanding of Australian law.
   c is an accurate reflection of Australian law.
   d reflects most people's understanding of the law.

6 Marysa thinks that refugee arrivals ...
   a increase the risk of terrorism.
   b need better protection from violence.
   c have been given thorough security checks.
   d understand the dangers of radicalism better than most.

7 Marysa thinks that strict immigration regulations ...
   a are inconvenient but necessary.
   b should be relaxed in cases of need.
   c are important for Australia's safety.
   d are more complicated than they should be.

3 PREPARING TO LISTEN: PREDICTING THE TOPIC

» SB, S108–109

Read task 4 'Is the Confederate flag offensive?' in the SB again, then answer the questions.

1 What kind of recording is it?

____

2 What subjects are definitely discussed in the podcast?

____

____

3 What key words might be in the podcast?

____

____

4 PREPARING TO LISTEN: QUESTIONS

5

A Read the questions below and in each one circle one key word or expression to listen for.

B In the podcast, US Americans discuss the Confederate flag. Listen and answer the questions below.

TIP

In this type of task, you must listen for specific details.

1 Jones claims that time are changing. What examples does she name? (*two examples*)

- ______________________________
- ______________________________

2 How do white people in the Southern states feel about the Confederate flag?

- ______________________________

3 How do people of colour in the southern USA feel about the flag? *(two aspects)*

- ______________________________
- ______________________________

4 What is the Confederate flag used instead of in some European countries?

- ______________________________

5 Why can the Confederate flag not be banned?

- ______________________________

SKILLS: READING

>> SB, SF4, S238

1 READING FOR GIST

>> SB, S102–105

Read the text 'Changing Nation' on page 41 quickly and tick the best summary.

a Immigration from eastern Europe has changed Britain. It has particularly benefitted the careers of female immigrants. Children seem to be integrating well. ☐

b Brexit put a stop to immigration from eastern Europe. Although their parents have done well in Britain, the children now want to return to eastern Europe. ☐

c Britain is used to dealing with waves of immigration. However, the integration of migrants takes a long time. Those who have worked hard to integrate have done well. ☐

2 UNDERSTANDING KEY VOCABULARY

Use a dictionary to write down the meaning of these expressions which are highlighted in the text, according to the context in which they are used.

a to dry up ______

b to reverse ______

c prospects ______

d upbeat ______

e progress ______

f executive ______

g enclave ______

h evenly ______

i roots ______

j to endure ______

3 ANSWERING QUESTIONS

A Read the questions in task 3B and find the paragraph(s) in the text which contain the information you need to answer each question.

Question 1 ______ Question 4 ______

Question 2 ______ Question 5 ______

Question 3 ______ Question 6 ______

B Read the text 'Changing Nation' on the next page, then answer the questions below.

1 What major demographic change occurred in the UK in the early 21st century?

______

2 How was Brexit expected to influence the situation?

______

3 What is unusual about the children of the eastern European immigrants?

______

4 In what respect are their mothers unusual?

______

5 Why else have the children integrated quickly?

6 What concerns their parents?

Changing Nation

[1] In 2004, the UK opened its borders to the new EU citizens of the 'EU8' countries: eight eastern European nations: Poland, Lithuania, Estonia, Latvia, the Czech Republic, Hungary, Slovakia and Slovenia.

[2] The UK government expected up to 13,000 immigrants to arrive each year. In the event, one-and-a-half million came in the first decade. It was one of the largest movements of people in Britain's history. By 2017, migrants from across the EU made up two million of the UK's 30 million workers, with non-EU immigration providing another million.

[3] As the 2020 deadline for Brexit loomed, and the status of EU citizens in the UK became uncertain, the flood of immigrants dried up. Yet it has not reversed direction as Europhiles feared and xenophobes hoped. The UK's 600,000 native Polish speakers are still the nation's largest linguistic minority. In 2021, seven out of 100 babies delivered in England and Wales were born to mothers from the EU8 countries.

[4] These statistics say little about the individuals who have come from the other end of Europe to make their home in Britain; less still about their children, many of whom were born in Britain and have known no other home. The migrants were drawn to the UK by the promise of good pay in exchange for hard work. Many found reasons to settle long-term: career advancement, a more comfortable lifestyle, a life partner, better prospects for their offspring, etc.

[5] Children of immigrants are often confused about their place in society. There is intergenerational tension when parents want to hold on tight to the culture of the old country but children are desperate to be accepted in the new. They may encounter xenophobia from locals and other migrant groups. These are common immigrant experiences across the world and, no doubt, throughout history.

[6] There are some aspects, though, that make the children of eastern European immigrants in the UK of the 2020s unusual, if not unique. In a nation struggling to find its place in the world after a messy exit from the European Union, and reeling from the COVID pandemic, anecdotal evidence suggests that these young people are surprisingly upbeat about their futures in the UK.

[7] One reason may be their parents – and particularly their mothers' – rapid economic progress. Many eastern European men had blue-collar skills which were in demand in Britain. Even if their English was not good, they quickly found well-paid employment as truck drivers, construction workers, plumbers, electricians and the like. For eastern European women, on the other hand, there was greater pressure to acquire fluent English and retrain. A Labour Force Survey from 2022 shows the result: UK women born in the EU8 are more likely to be executives and professionals than men from those countries. They are role models to their children, especially their daughters.

[8] Another factor is geographical distribution. Earlier waves of immigrants from the Commonwealth tended to settle in enclaves, producing locally high concentrations of their ethnic group. Eastern European immigrants followed the jobs – to whatever part of the UK offered the best prospects. As a result, these families are distributed much more evenly across the country and the children are less likely to have peers from their home country in their classes, sports clubs and social groups.

[9] This is not necessarily what the parents want. They may enrol their children in Saturday schools where the culture and language of their home country is taught, so that the children don't 'lose their roots'. Informal reports suggest that many of the children endure this rather than embracing it. They see their future as British and besides, what child wants an extra weekly dose of school?

(607 words)

SKILLS: TRANSLATION (ENGLISH–GERMAN)

>>SB, SF11, S252

1 DEN TEXT ÜBERFLIEGEN

>>SB, S102–105

Überfliegen Sie den Text auf Seite 43, um sich einen Überblick zu verschaffen. Welche Zusammenfassung des Texts passt am besten?

a Der Text setzt sich mit den Gründen auseinander, warum Menschen ihre Heimat verlassen. ☐

b Der Text beschreibt, wie Migration zu Spannungen führen kann, und plädiert für Toleranz. ☐

c Der Text beschreibt die Vor- und Nachteile einer multikulturellen Gesellschaft. ☐

2 VOKABELN MIT MEHREREN ÜBERSETZUNGSMÖGLICHKEITEN

Wie sind die fettgedruckten Wörter am treffendsten zu übersetzen?

1 The refugees feel **vulnerable** in their new country.
- a anfällig ☐
- b schwach ☐
- c schutzlos ☐

2 The ethnic **make-up** of our communities has changed.
- a Make-up ☐
- b Veranlagung ☐
- c Zusammensetzung ☐

3 This is **true** for both the hosts and the new arrivals.
- a echt ☐
- b tatsächlich ☐
- c zutreffend ☐

4 It is a challenge to **deal with** big social changes.
- a behandeln ☐
- b fertig werden mit ☐
- c sich kümmern um ☐

3 FESTSTEHENDE AUSDRÜCKE

Wie sind diese feststehenden Ausdrücke aus dem Text am besten ins Deutsche zu übersetzen?

1 to some extent ______________________________

2 after all ______________________________

3 as a result of ______________________________

4 find one's feet ______________________________

5 at the same time ______________________________

6 to face pressure ______________________________

4 ING-FORM → ZU + INFINITIV

Vervollständigen Sie die Übersetzungen mit zu + Infinitiv des Verbs in Klammern.

1 They have difficulty integrating. (*sich integrieren*)

Sie haben Schwierigkeiten damit, ______________________

2 Holding on to their culture is important for them. (*behalten*)

Es ist wichtig für sie, ______________________

3 It's a way of keeping their identity. (*sich etw erhalten*)

Es ist ein Mittel, ______________________

5 DIE ÜBERSETZUNG SCHREIBEN

Übersetzen Sie den Text ins Deutsche. Bleiben Sie mit Ihrer Version möglichst nah am Original, aber formulieren Sie trotzdem so, dass es nicht wie eine Übersetzung klingt.

The challenges of immigration

All nations in Europe are multicultural to some extent. After all, modern Europeans are the product of thousands of years of migration. Changes in the ethnic make-up of our communities have accelerated in the past 100 years, as political and economic factors have driven millions of people to leave their homelands and look for a new life and new opportunities in a foreign country.

In this situation, culture clashes are likely to happen. Conservative communities are wary of new influences, so that outsiders find it difficult to gain acceptance. There have been cases where a warm initial welcome was later replaced by tension and suspicion, as new waves of immigrants followed. When people feel that their way of life is threatened, they frequently look for safety within their group – this is true for both the new arrivals and their hosts. In the worst cases, this has led to hatred, violence and persecution.

Immigrants often feel vulnerable in their new country. Some will have left their homeland reluctantly, so it is understandable if they have difficulty finding their feet in unfamiliar surroundings. While most are grateful to their host countries, they may not want to integrate fully into the new society. Perhaps they cannot because of language and cultural barriers. Holding on to the customs and culture of one's home country is a way of keeping one's identity.

The children of this immigrant generation often find it difficult to discover their own cultural identity. They experience discrimination because of their background and at the same time face pressure from their families not to give up the culture of their homeland, including their religion and language. They may feel that they belong to both countries – or neither.

It is a challenge for any society to deal with large-scale change. On the other hand, change is unavoidable, so isn't it better to face it with hope and optimism, rather than resist it?

(319 words)

9 The state and politics

WORKING WITH WORDS

1 SOCIETY AND ECONOMICS

» SB, S114–117

Complete the sentences with the most appropriate word from the box. There are more words than you need.

aged • ageist • birth • boost • career • labour • priority • retirement • security • shortage • societal

1 One answer to a long-term skills ______________ is to increase immigration.
2 By 2029 the official ______________ age will be 67.
3 According to the latest ______________ market statistics, there are many unfilled job vacancies.
4 After the Second World War, there was a baby boom in Europe as the ______________ rate shot up.
5 With more of us living longer, more money will need to be spent on ______________ care.
6 Most people who are out of work have to rely on social ______________ payments.
7 Rather than taking early retirement at 55, she chose a complete ______________ change.
8 Our ageing population will become a serious ______________ issue if we do not address it now.

2 CRIMINAL JUSTICE: VERBS

» SB, S118–121

Complete the text with verbs from the box. You may need to change the form of some verbs. There is one verb that you do not need.

break • discourage • ensure • guard • lock • normalize • protect • punish • reduce • release • reward • serve • take • threaten • treat

The criminal justice system has many functions. It decides who ______________ [1] the law. It ______________ [2] criminals and it ______________ [3] society from them by ______________ [4] them in a secure place. More generally it ______________ [5] good citizenship and ______________ [6] anti-social behaviour by ______________ [7] would-be criminals with unpleasant consequences. The decision to ______________ [8] away a person's liberty and ______________ [9] them up must not be taken lightly. In almost all cases the justice system ______________ [10] prisoners back into society after they ______________ [11] their sentences. If we want them to behave like good citizens after their release, we need to ______________ [12] them like human beings while they are in prison. The system needs to ______________ [13] inmates for good behaviour. It follows that prison is not society's 'revenge' on the criminal – and to treat it as such ______________ [14] public safety rather than increasing it.

3 COMPOUND NOUNS

» SB, S122–125

Join words from A and words from B to make pairs. Then write a sentence with each of them in your exercise book.

A border • career • cross-border • economic • labour • member • national • passport • personal

B borders • checks • freedom • market • opportunities • power • restrictions • states • travel

GRAMMAR

1 VERB + INFINITIVE *VS* VERB + –ING (1)

» SB, S115; GF15, S267

Complete the sentences with the correct form of the verb in brackets.

1 Do you think many parents regret ______________ children? (have)
2 Some older people would prefer ______________ at work as long as possible. (stay)
3 For decades, politicians have avoided ______________ with the issue. (deal)
4 How can Germany manage ______________ more skilled migrants? (attract)
5 The government refused ______________ the state pension. (reduce)
6 Should Germany consider ______________ the retirement age? (raise)
7 It is not that people forget ______________ children – they simply do not want them. (have)
8 Most people hope ______________ fit and active in their old age. (remain)

2 VERB + INFINITIVE *VS* VERB + –ING (2)

» SB, S115; GF15, S267

Write each verb from task 1 in the correct place in the diagram. Then add the verbs in the box.

afford • begin • choose • continue • decide • deny • dislike • enjoy • expect • hate • imagine • like • love • miss • start

+ infinitive	both	+ -ing

3 PRESENT PERFECT AND SIMPLE PAST

» SB, S123; GF03, GF05, S259

Complete the text with the correct forms of the verbs in brackets.

Brexit ______________ 1 (be) the withdrawal of the United Kingdom from the European Union on 31 January 2020. The UK is the only sovereign country which ______________ 2 (leave) the EU since its founding.

The UK ______________ 3 (join) the European Economic Community (EEC) in 1973. Twenty years later the EEC ______________ 4 (become) the European Union (EU) when the Maastricht Treaty ______________ 5 (come) into force. The UK and the other 11 original members of the EU ______________ 6 (sign) the treaty and since then 16 more countries ______________ 7 (join) the EU.

The institutions and aims of the EU ______________ 8 (develop) significantly since 1993, and some British Eurosceptics ______________ 9 (claim) in 2016 that the EU ______________ 10 (be) no longer the organization that the UK ______________ 11 (sign) up for in 1973 and 1993. There ______________ 12 (always be) a strong Eurosceptic element in British politics. However, when the Prime Minister of the day, David Cameron, ______________ 13 (agree) to hold a referendum on continued EU membership in 2016, he ______________ 14 (expect) that there would be a clear vote in favour of staying in the EU. His government ______________ 15 (be) strongly in favour of the UK's continued membership. But the British people ______________ 16 (vote) to leave the EU by a narrow majority (51.9%).

SKILLS: LISTENING

>>SB, SF05, S240

1 PREPARING TO LISTEN: UNDERSTANDING THE GIST

» SB, S114–117

Match the headings A–F with the quotations 1 to 6.

A Poverty affects self-esteem and mental health. ☐
B Income stress is linked to violence in the home. ☐
C Poverty causes various social and health issues. ☐
D Poverty is linked to poor educational outcomes. ☐
E Poor-quality housing affects health. ☐
F Poverty causes nutritional problems. ☐

1 'It's basically just junk food – but it's cheap and it's filling.'
2 'Nobody wants me here. Dad would be better off without me.'
3 'I'd like to stay in school, but Mum needs me to get a job.'
4 'Mum and Dad often fight about money.'
5 'It puts young people at risk in a multitude of ways.'
6 'It's disgusting here and we feel sick all the time.'

2 MULTIPLE MATCHING

6

You are going to hear four people talking about childhood poverty in the UK.

While listening, match the headings A–F with the speakers 1–4. There are two more headings than you need.

A Poverty affects self-esteem and mental health.
B Income stress is linked to violence in the home.
C Poverty causes various social and health issues.
D Poverty is linked to poor educational outcomes.
E Poor-quality housing affects health.
F Poverty causes nutritional problems.

Tip
In this type of task, you must listen for gist – the main ideas expressed in the recording. Your answers to task 1 will help you.

Speaker	1	2	3	4
Heading				

Statements not used: ________ ________

3 PREPARING TO LISTEN: KEY WORDS

>> SB, S118–121

Read the questions in task 4 below from a multiple choice listening task. Circle or highlight the key words in each sentence.

4 MULTIPLE CHOICE

7

You are going to hear a podcast discussion about the police in the USA.

Tip

In this type of task, you must listen for specific details. Your answers to task 3 will help you.

Listen and choose the correct answer for each question. There is only one correct answer.

1 Police forces in the USA are run ...
   a as private businesses.
   b by the federal government.
   c by the state or local government area.
   d according to strict national guidelines.

2 According to Troy Rivers, US police training ...
   a is too short and superficial.
   b focuses on the wrong skills.
   c is conducted mostly by military instructors.
   d focuses excessively on weapons training.

3 In potentially violent situations, many US police are trained to ...
   a defend themselves effectively.
   b shoot first and ask questions later.
   c use fear to make people follow orders.
   d use psychological techniques to avoid the use of force.

4 According to Alicia Morales, the police should...
   a pay their employees less.
   b have their spending reduced.
   c do a better job with the funds they have.
   d receive more money from the government.

5 Morales believes that public safety would be improved by ...
   a arresting more criminals.
   b closing some police departments.
   c spending money in different areas.
   d making the police more supportive of local communities.

6 International evidence shows that social reforms are ...
   a likely to increase crime rates.
   b largely unrelated to crime rates.
   c idealistic unless crime is reduced first.
   d the most effective way of reducing crime.

7 Aggressive policing is ineffective because ...
   a it causes criminals to use more violence.
   b it harms the local communities.
   c it is too expensive to maintain in the longer term.
   d it spreads the message that violence is acceptable.

SKILLS: MEDIATION (ENGLISH-GERMAN)

>> SB S118–121; SF10, S250

SITUATION: Sie sind Mitglied einer Jugendgruppe, die sich an einem Projekt für bürgernahe Polizeiarbeit beteiligt.

AUFGABE: Erstellen Sie für Ihre Gruppe ein Infoblatt über den Einsatz unbewaffneter Polizeistreifen, indem Sie folgende Aspekte aus dem Zeitungsartikel auf Seite 49 zusammenfassen:
- Vorteile unbewaffneter Polizeistreifen
- ihre Methoden im Umgang mit potenziell gewalttätigen Auseinandersetzungen
- Voraussetzungen für den Einsatz von Waffen bei der Polizei

1 DIE AUFGABE ANALYSIEREN

Ursprungstext: *Armed police: friend or foe?*

Mediationstext
- Adressat: ______
- Medium/Textsorte: ______
- Zweck: ______
- Sprachebene: ______

2 DEN INHALT ANALYSIEREN

A Tragen Sie in die Tabelle die Nummern jener Absätze des Textes auf Seite 49 ein, in denen diese Themen behandelt werden (= Spalte A).

Thema	A Absatz	B Relevanz	C Bulletpoint
wie sich US Polizeistreifen Gehorsam verschaffen	*10*		
Länder, in denen Polizeistreifen unbewaffnet sind			
'Policing by consent': Definition			
Vorgehensweise unbewaffneter Streifen bei potenziell gewalttätigen Auseinandersetzungen			
der leichte Zugang zu Schusswaffen in den USA und dessen Folgen für die Polizei			
Verhältnis zwischen Bewaffnung der Polizei u. Waffenkriminalität			
Todesfälle-Statistik: Länder mit bewaffneten Polizeistreifen			
Todesfälle-Statistik: Länder mit unbewaffneten Polizeistreifen			

B Welche der Themen sind für Ihre Aufgabe relevant? Haken (√) Sie diese ab (= Spalte B).

C Ordnen Sie die gewählten Themen den drei Bulletpoints in der Aufgabe oben zu (Bulletpoint 1: Vorteile unbewaffneter Polizeistreifen usw.).

3 VERFASSEN DER MEDIATION

Schreiben Sie nun Ihr Infoblatt.

Armed police: friend or foe?

[1] Police policy on firearms varies widely around the globe. Nineteen countries do not arm police officers for their routine duties. Most are small islands, but others include the United Kingdom (except Northern Ireland), Ireland, South Korea and New Zealand.

[2] These countries have average gun-crime rates which are lower than countries where the police are armed. This is consistent and seems to be a matter of causation, not just correlation.

[3] In Germany, police routinely carry firearms. Although their use is strictly regulated, most years ten to twenty civilians are killed by German police bullets.

[4] Around six thousand British police are authorised to carry guns when required, and there are around 15,000 incidents each year requiring the attendance of armed police. Yet the annual deaths across the UK as a result of police gun use are generally *five or fewer* in a country of 69 million inhabitants. In some years, nobody is killed.

[5] In the USA, by contrast, over one thousand people are shot dead by police every year, out of a population only five times that of the UK.

[6] Statistics can only tell us so much. Equally important, although difficult to quantify, is society's understanding of the role of the police force. This affects the way that police are trained, the way that they behave towards the public, and how the public regards them.

[7] The modern philosophy of policing in the UK was developed in the early 19th century after a number of killings by police, including the Peterloo Massacre of 1819, where soldiers and police on horses charged repeatedly into a crowd of peaceful pro-democracy protesters.

[8] After these terrible events, a new approach was developed: 'policing by consent'. Police officers were to understand themselves as citizens in uniform, whose authority derived from the public's consent and co-operation. Police forces in many English-speaking countries, including Ireland, Canada and Australia, are based on this principle.

[9] Policing by consent affects how police officers are trained. Training of British police emphasises de-escalation – how to defuse potentially violent confrontations using practical psychology and cultural awareness. If the person is carrying a gun or other lethal weapon, highly trained armed police can usually be called in within minutes.

[10] The standard approach in the USA, by contrast, seems to be to escalate the threat of force, and then the *actual use* of force, until compliance is achieved – or, in too many cases, the person dies. Being stopped by police in the USA, even for a routine traffic check, is often described as a terrifying, traumatic experience, particularly for people of colour.

[11] A better approach is needed, but will not be easy to implement. Different circumstances require different policing. Officers in the USA, where guns are freely available, have to assume that the person they are questioning is armed and that their own life is in danger. This fundamentally changes the relationship between public and police.

(487 words)

10 A globalized world

WORKING WITH WORDS

1 ADJECTIVE + NOUN COLLOCATIONS

» SB, S130–133

Complete the text with eight of the ten collocations in the box.

backbreaking loads • constant fear • damning report • guilty conscience • human rights • terrible blow • illegal miners • moral obligation • raw materials • unique code

Everyone has a mobile phone but no one thinks about the ________ ________ [1] such as cobalt and copper that are used in them and where they come from. Before Amnesty International published its ________ ________ [2] about cobalt in 2016, most consumers had no idea that a lot of it comes from the DRC, and that it is mined by children working deep underground, carrying ________ ________ [3] of up to 40 kg and living in ________ ________ [4] of being buried alive in a landslide. The sad reality is that unscrupulous international traders without a ________ ________ [5] regularly abuse the ________ ________ [6] of the DRC's 150,000 ________ ________ [7]. So will we, as consumers, now feel a ________ ________ [8] to find out how our phones, tablets and laptops are made and only buy ethically sourced goods? Time will tell …

2 PREPOSITIONS

» SB, S134–136

Complete the text with prepositions from the box. They can all be found in the text on page 134 of the SB.

about • by (2x) • in (2x) • of (2x) • with

Let's face it, before we make a decision ________ [1] buying something, we probably check the price on Amazon because Amazon is a treasure trove ________ [2] information where you can find almost anything you want. Its expertise ________ [3] data collection and analysis is legendary and this makes it beloved ________ [4] consumers all over the world. Amazon has a finger ________ [5] every pie except real estate and is obsessed ________ [6] finding out exactly what its customers want. However, it is feared ________ [7] some businesses and accused ________ [8] copying their products and selling them at half the price.

3 WORD FAMILIES

» SB, S138–139

A Look at the text on page 138 of the SB to fill in the gaps in the table.

	Verb	Noun (abstract)	Noun (person/thing)	Adjective
1	to	reference	referee	referable
2	to familiarize	familiarity	X	
3	to economize		economist	
4	to	growth	grower	X
5	to	advice	adviser	advisable

B Choose a word from each word family (1–5) in A to complete the sentences. Make any necessary changes.

1 Confusingly, 'Road' in China's Belt and Road Initiative ______________ to sea routes.

2 Chinese people are now coming to Duisburg to ______________ themselves with life in Germany.

3 ______________ agree that energy should no longer come from fossil fuels like coal.

4 They say that that economic ______________ will come from the service sector and not from manufacturing.

5 Their ______________ to cities like Duisburg is to focus on transport and trade.

GRAMMAR

1 PAST PERFECT AND SIMPLE PAST

» SB, S131; GF3, S259, GF7, S260

Complete the text with verbs in the simple past or the past perfect. Use the simple past to go forwards in the story and use the past perfect to go backwards in time or with 'after' and 'as soon as'.

Early last Monday morning, Mrs Miles ______________ [1] (drive) to the EatNow Food Bank, ______________ [2] (get) out of her car and ______________ [3] (carry) the big box of fruit and vegetables that a local supermarket ______________ [4] (donate) into the storeroom. She ______________ [5] (drive) to all the nearby supermarkets the day before and some of them ______________ [6] (have) some food left over. After she ______________ [7] (put) down the box, she ______________ [8] (say) hello to Sally, who ______________ [9] (be) in the shop since 7 a.m. and ______________ [10] (go) to the entrance. There ______________ [11] (be) a long queue of people waiting outside and as soon as she ______________ [12] (unlock) the door, they all ______________ [13] (come) streaming in. Some of them ______________ [14] (be) very hungry because they ______________ [15] (not eat) for several days.

2 REPORTED SPEECH: REPORTING VERB IN THE PAST

» SB, S140; GF12, S263

Make all necessary changes to turn the sentences into reported speech.

	Direct speech	Reported speech (reporting verb in the past)
1	Tina: 'I live in Duisburg.'	Tina said she ______________ in Duisburg.
2	'I don't work for a German company.'	She said she ______________ for a German company.
3	'I worked for Schmidt KG for 20 years.'	She said she ______________ for Schmidt KG for 20 years.
4	'I've been working for Wang Ltd for six months.	She said she ______________ for Wang Ltd for six months.
5	'I'll stay at Wang Ltd for the time being.	She said she ______________ at Wang Ltd for the time being.
6	'Where do you work, Tim?'	She asked Tim where he ______________.
7	'Did you work for a big firm when you lived in London?'	She asked ______________ he ______________ for a big firm when he lived in London.
8	'Do you have to you start work early?'	She asked ______________ he ______________ start work early.
9	Tim: 'Please tell me about the job interview tomorrow, Tina.'	Tim ______________ Tina ______________ him about the job interview ______________.
10	Tim: 'Don't tell my boss, Tina!'	Tim ______________ Tina ______________ his boss.

SKILLS: LISTENING

» SB, SF05, S240

1 PREPARING TO LISTEN: KEY WORDS

» SB, S130–133

A Group the words in the box below under the headings in the table.

ashamed • children • conflict • dignity • extreme weather conditions • human rights • humiliating • old people • political conflicts • proud • rationing • refugees • settle disputes • shortages • single parents • sustainability

Emotions and feelings	People in need	Problems in supermarkets	Supply chain factors
1	1	1	1
2	2	2	2
3	3	3	3
4	4	4	4

B Which four words in A match with the definitions below?

a	making you feel ashamed and stupid
b	people who have been forced to leave their homes because of war, etc.
c	not enough of something
d	use of products in a way that does not harm the environment

2 MULTIPLE MATCHING

8

You are going to hear four people talking about globalization and how it affects them.

While listening, match the headings A to F with the speakers 1 to 4. There are two more headings than you need.

A Banks on track to make huge profits
B Long supply chains a thing of the past
C Pensioner's pain and shame
D Rising prices hit young and old
E Shoppers battle for basics in supermarkets
F Taxes expected to rise again

Speaker	1	2	3	4
Heading				

Headings not used: ____________

3 LISTENING FOR INFORMATION

» SB, S130–133

9

You are going to hear a radio programme in which the mayor of a town answers questions about what is happening to the town centre and what can be done about it.

Only use information from the broadcast to complete the tasks.

A Fill in each gap with a word from the broadcast.

1 Mayor: The problem with our town centre is that it is ______________________.

2 Mayor: Years ago the town centre was crowded but nowadays it's just an empty ______________________.

3 Interviewer: Some people say that shops are closing because of global online ______________________.

4 Mayor: One global giant is ______________________ physical shops.

5 Mayor: Shops need to offer a ______________________ service with both offline and online sales.

B Tick (✓) two solutions suggested by the mayor from the following list.

1 help local businesses to compete by offering them cheap credit ☐

2 set up a regional online sales platform ☐

3 lower shop rents ☐

4 make the minimum shop rental period five years ☐

5 attract more large department stores to the town centre ☐

C Circle the correct option.

1 Town centres all look the same because …

a all the shops open and shut at the same time.

b the street lighting isn't bright enough to attract people in the evening.

c you always see the same fast food restaurants and chain stores.

d there is nowhere to park and public transport is poor.

2 A coworking space is a central office location …

a with free coffee, a TV and comfortable armchairs and sofas.

b that people can easily reach by public transport or bike.

c located in a hotel, so people can spend the night there if they work late.

d with basic office furniture, internet and printing facilities and a café nearby.

3 One way to solve the problem of litter caused by throw-away plastic packaging is to …

a ban all takeaway food.

b tax all snack bars and restaurants selling food to go.

c employ more road-sweepers in the city centre.

d make anyone caught throwing away plastic packaging pay a heavy fine.

D Complete the answer to the following question. Write a short sentence.

What can be done to make the town centre more attractive?

- There need to be more cafés and pubs.
- ____

SKILLS: READING

» SB; SF1, S248; SF5, S256

1 COMPREHENSION

Read the text below and do the tasks on page 55.

Globalization RIP – Long live globalization!

For many, globalization is a dirty word, but it wasn't always like that. In the late 19th century, Britain used its strong navy and vast empire to dominate world trade and start the globalization process. After World War II, the USA took over and China followed in the 1990s and early 2000s. Globalization created wealth, lifted people out of poverty and reduced inequality between countries. It was highly visible in the form of containers of goods, vehicles and machinery being shipped all over the world to both developed and developing countries, boosting economies and improving the quality of many people's lives.

In the 1960s, advances in new media technologies, such as radio and television, made it possible for people to sit at home in their living rooms in one country and simultaneously experience events taking place in others, for example the 1964 Tokyo Olympics were watched by 400 million people.

The world was 'a global village', and western food, fashion, cars and culture – music in particular – reached almost every corner of the planet and even in communist eastern Europe it was chic to wear American jeans and T-shirts designed in San Francisco and sewn in Sri Lanka. Instead of national governments, international organizations, such as the International Monetary Fund (IMF) founded in 1945, the Organisation for Economic Co-operation and Development (OECD, 1961) and the World Trade Organization (WTO, 1995), defined 'the rules of the game', and free trade crossed political and ideological boundaries as never before.

Then, at the end of the 1990s, the tide started to turn. In 1999 the first serious anti-globalization protests took place at the WTO meeting in Seattle in Canada and became known as the 'Battle of Seattle'. Protesters fought police in the streets, smashed shops and cars, and hundreds were arrested. They blamed globalization for exploiting the poor in developing countries and the low-skilled in advanced economies and for causing environmental damage. They now also blame it for the Covid-19 pandemic.

Nevertheless, from the late 1990s until 2007 globalization boomed and world trade grew by 6% per year. Then, in 2008, the worldwide financial crisis struck, there was an abrupt downturn and, according to WTO estimates, world trade shrank by 2%, losing trillions of dollars on the world's stock markets. After a slow recovery in the next decade, disaster struck again in 2020 with the outbreak of Covid-19. The IMF's figures show that world trade contracted again, but this time by a massive 9%. Among the many consequences were geopolitical tensions between the West and China (where the pandemic is believed to have originated) and protectionism (America first!) whereby developed countries only vaccinated their own populations and left the poor in other continents to fend for themselves.

So is globalization a thing of the past? While this may be true for old-style globalization, meaning trade in visible goods, new-style 'invisible' trade in the form of cross-border data transfers is expanding exponentially with a yearly growth rate of up to 20% since 2005. This astonishing growth rate is due to the increasing use of cloud computing, the rise of big data, and the growing popularity of internet-based services such as social media and e-commerce. And it isn't just data that's criss-crossing the globe: new-style globalization flows are also financial. According to the OECD, foreign direct investment, i.e. financing subsidiaries, joint ventures and real estate abroad and buying shares in foreign companies, is back to where it was before the financial crisis. So, in a nutshell, globalization is back with a vengeance but invisible to the naked eye. (600 words)

A Mark the following statements true (T) or false (F). Justify your answers with line numbers.

		T/F	Line numbers
1	Globalization has always been unpopular.		
2	The last big anti-globalization protests were over 20 years ago in Seattle.		
3	Many anti-globalization protesters believe that globalization caused the Covid-19 pandemic.		

B Complete the sentences below with words from lines 16 to 20 of the text.

At the 'Battle of Seattle', anti-globalization ______________________ [1] wanted to tell the world that globalization was causing suffering and hardship to ______________________ [2] people in rich countries and poor people in ______________________ [3] countries. They also believed it had caused great ______________________ [4] to the environment. There was so much fighting that the police ______________________ [5] large numbers of people.

C List the advantages and disadvantages of globalization according to the views put forward in the text. Your answers may be in note form.

Advantages:

____

Disadvantages:

____

D Outline the difference between visible and invisible trade in no more than 60 words. Write whole sentences.

____

E Match the ideas expressed in the text (1–3) below with the organizations (IMF, OECD, WTO).

IMF (International Monetary Fund)
OECD (Organisation for Economic Co-operation and Development)
WTO (World Trade Organization)

1	The 2008 financial crisis led to a huge downturn in trade and huge losses on the world's stock markets.	
2	World trade contracted by 9% in 2020.	
3	Big companies and governments are still investing very large sums of money in foreign countries to finance commercial ventures.	

F Show the order of the events referred to in the text by writing A, B, C and D next to the corresponding dates in the table.

A financial crisis
B boom in cross-border data transfers
C British domination of world trade
D boom in globalization

1880–1899	
1998/9–2007	
since 2005	
2008	

G Explain the meaning of the following numbers as they are used in the text.

1961 ____________________

____

2% ____________________

____

20% ____________________

____

H The text concludes by saying that 'globalization is back with a vengeance' (lines 39–40). List the facts that support this opinion. (Answers in note form permitted).

____

____

____

____

SKILLS: WRITING

>> SB, SF6, S242; SF7, S244

After a project week at your college about the pros and cons of globalization you get an email from your Irish penfriend Fiona asking your opinion about getting an expensive new mobile phone. You write back to her. Start your email as shown below and finish with *Love*, ... or *Best wishes*, ... (your first name).

> Hey Fiona,
> I was really interested to hear that you're getting a new smartphone. There are lots to choose from but have you thought about a fair-trade phone? In my opinion, ...

1 GATHERING INFORMATION

Choose the smartphone features that you think are important from the list. Add your own ideas.

	conventional smartphone	fair-trade smartphone
Average price	€1,000	€600
5-year support	✓	✓
recyclable materials; low-waste manufacturing		✓
Ethical supply chain		✓
Guarantee	2 years	5 years
Must-have fashion accessory and status symbol	✓	
No child labour; good working conditions for workers		✓
Price of parts and repairs (battery, display, camera etc.)	expensive	affordable
Removable battery		✓
Self-repair	voids guarantee	✓
Special tools and skills needed for repairs	✓	none

2 USEFUL PHRASES

Choose expressions from the table to link your ideas.

Introducing ideas	Listing ideas	Stating results
It's important to remember that ... We shouldn't forget that ... We shouldn't only think about ...	First of all, ... Secondly, ... Finally, ...	The result is that ... As a consequence, ... This leads to ...

Contrasting ideas	Useful words	Closing
On the one hand, ... On the other hand, ... Some ... (e.g. employers) but others ... Whereas ... (e.g. we have strict laws), some countries ...	Furthermore, ... Nowadays, ... However, ...	All in all, ... In a nutshell, ... In the long term, ...

3 WRITING THE COMPOSITION

Write your composition in your exercise book. Write about 150 words.

11 Science and technology

WORKING WITH WORDS

1 OPPOSITES

>> SB, S146–147

Find opposites of the words below. The answers are in the text on pages 146–147 of the SB.

1	necessary		**6**	public	
2	rare		**7**	unwilling	
3	true		**8**	honest	
4	correct		**9**	high	
5	tiny		**10**	delighted	

2 ADJECTIVES FROM NOUNS

>> SB, S150–151

A **Form adjectives from the nouns in the table below. Three end in *-ous*, three in *-ble* and four in *-al*. Use the text on pages 150–151 of the SB and a dictionary if necessary.**

	Noun	Adjective		Noun	Adjective
1	population		**6**	error	
2	flexibility		**7**	technology	
3	environment		**8**	autonomy	
4	psychology		**9**	fatalities	
5	avoidance		**10**	value	

B **Use the words in A as adjectives or adverbs to complete the text.**

>> SB, S150–151; GF15, S268

In ____________ [1] cities, such as Delhi or Jakarta with over 30 million people, the toxic emissions from cars and trucks are a huge ____________ [2] problem. Large numbers of vehicles also produce stress and many people report having ____________ [3] problems due to the noise and danger of the traffic. And they have good reason to feel stressed, because last year in Delhi, for example, 3.6% more people were ____________ [4] injured in road accidents with more than 1,200 people killed. Some scientists believe that ____________ [5] vehicles, such as driverless buses and cars, could be the answer. Others say that that such vehicles could never respond as ____________ [6] as a human driver because they cannot react quickly to unexpected situations. However, the good news is that most accidents are ____________ [7] because they are caused by human error and it is to be hoped that advances in artificial intelligence will help scientists find a ____________ [8] solution to a very human problem.

3 WORD FIELD: GENETIC ENGINEERING

» SB, S154–155

Complete the text with the following words from pages 154–155 of the SB.

breakthrough • chemotherapy • diagnosed • drug-resistant • genetically • infusion • incurable • leukaemia • marrow • molecular scissors • palliative care • treatment

The medical definition of ______________ [1] is cancer of the white blood cells. The illness begins inside the patient's bones in the bone ______________ [2] and anyone who is ______________ [3] with this disease knows that the ______________ [4] will take about two years and will include several rounds of ______________ [5], whereby drugs are given to stop the cancer cells from growing and spreading. In Layla Richard's case, the drugs didn't work. Her parents were told that her cancer was ______________ [6] and that she only had a short time to live. The doctors suggested giving her ______________ [7] for the last few months of her life, but luckily for Leyla, scientists at the hospital were working on an entirely new way of treating cancer that involved editing genes using ______________ [8]. She was given a 1 ml ______________ [9] of ______________ [10] engineered cells and a few weeks later the cancer had stopped. Leyla's success story was a ______________ [11] for modern medicine and offers great hope to people suffering from ______________ [12] cancers.

GRAMMAR

1 IF-SENTENCES

» SB, S148; GF14, S266

A Complete the if-sentences with the verbs in brackets.

1 If scientists find a cure for cancer, many sufferers all over the world ______________ (survive).
2 If they ______________ (not get) treatment early, their chances of recovery won't be so good.
3 If people ______________ (smoke) less, there wouldn't be so many cases of lunger cancer.
4 If parents didn't smoke, their children ______________ (not live) in a smokey atmosphere.
5 If scientists hadn't experimented with gene-editing, they ______________ (not cure) Layla.
6 If they ______________ (not give) Layla a special new drug, she wouldn't have survived.

B Complete the text with the verbs in brackets.

If scientists ______________ [1] (not discover) the structure of DNA in in 1953, many scientists ______________ [2] (not understand) how the human body works. Doctors now know that if they ______________ [3] (treat) certain types of cancer with gene therapy, the patients ______________ [4] (survive). If every hospital ______________ [5] (have) access to this expensive technology, far more patients ______________ [6] (make) a full recovery, but this is unlikely to happen for financial reasons.

SKILLS: READING

» SB, SF1, S248; SF5, S256

1 COMPREHENSION

Read the text below and do the tasks in the table on page 61.

Are anti-vaxxers a thing of the past? British reporter Toby Simpson toured the US to find out

Since 2020 over 500,000 people have died in the USA as a result of the Covid-19 pandemic. The internet was initially flooded with the wildest of conspiracy theories but then the pharmaceutical industry went into top gear and produced some highly effective vaccines, so have views now changed?

I started my journey in Florida, America's sunshine state, but it was all doom and gloom when I spoke to retiree Margaret Trent (72) about her views on vaccines. 'I stay clear of them!' she said. 'They were rushed out without proper testing and they change your genes! Once they're in your DNA anything can happen! And they give kids autism!' She added that her views were supported by one ex-president and all her family and friends felt the same.

In the French Quarter of New Orleans, I got chatting to Ella Jackson (32) at the next table in a restaurant and when I mentioned the article I was writing, her reply was simple: 'Anyone who's young and healthy has no need to get vaccinated for Covid.' She added that her husband had tested positive with no symptoms at all and then wasted a week in quarantine. She wore a mask in shops and on public transport, disinfected her hands regularly and fist-bumped instead of shaking hands and as vaccines wore off after a few months anyway, she didn't see the point.

I next spoke to Dr Sydney Scott (56) at a world-renowned hospital in Phoenix, Arizona. He told me he had been horrified by anti-vaxxers' posts on social media saying that vaccines changed your DNA and Covid was no more serious than flu. In 2020 there had been 25,000 deaths from flu in the USA but over 350,000 from Covid. He explained that the new vaccines used RNA, not DNA, to carry information to the body's immune system to enable it to combat Covid, and as RNA could only survive at low temperatures, it died in the body a few days later. The rapid development of the new vaccines was because the pandemic had made it easy to find the 44,000 participants needed for trials, so emergency authorization had been granted in less than a year. As for autism, the English doctor who had made that claim was corrupt and had lost his licence.

Dr Scott then put me in contact with one of his patients, Ted Blunt (47). He had been a convinced anti-vaxxer, going on demos and posting radical views on social media until December 2020, when he caught Covid. He suddenly had severe chest pain and great difficulty breathing. His skin went blue and he was rushed to hospital and put on a ventilator. He survived but ever since he has suffered from extreme fatigue. More worryingly, he also has brain fog. His advice to everyone now is: 'Get yourself vaccinated!' (500 words)

1 COMPREHENSION

Read the text and complete the table below in English.

1 Why did Toby Simpson believe that Americans' attitudes towards vaccination might have changed?	
2 What were Margaret Trent's fears regarding Covid vaccines? *(3 aspects)*	• • •
3 How does Ella Jackson deal with the threat of Covid? *(3 aspects)*	• • •
4 What was Dr Scott's reason for classifying Covid as a serious illness compared to the flu?	
5 How does RNA have a vital but short-lived role in the new vaccines?	
6 Why was it possible to grant emergency authorization for the new vaccines in such a short time?	
7 What happened to Ted Blunt that he ceased being an anti-vaxxer?	

2 MULTIPLE MATCHING

Match the ideas A to F with the people interviewed. There are two more ideas than you need.

A Covid is really only bad for old people.

B Everyone should be vaccinated as soon as possible.

C Hospitals need more ventilators.

D Modern vaccines do not affect the body's DNA.

E Quarantine should be for at least a week.

F Vaccines harm your health.

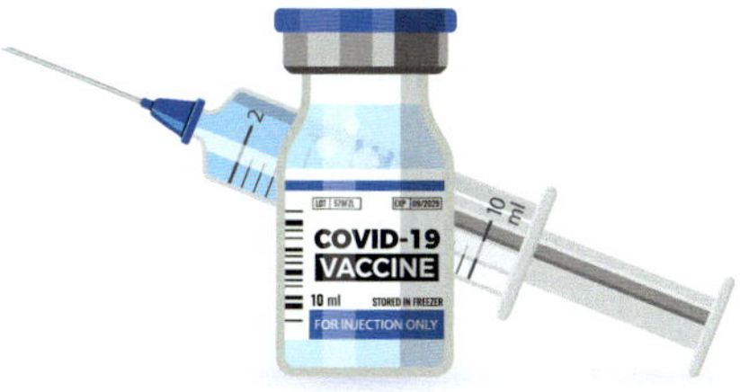

	Margaret Trent	Ella Jackson	Sydney Scott	Ted Blunt
Idea				

Headings not used: __________

SKILLS: MEDIATION (ENGLISH–GERMAN)

» SB, SF6, SB PP. 258–259

In einem Online-Forum für Schülerinnen und Schüler wird darüber diskutiert, wie digitale Antworten auf den demografischen Wandel und die Pflege-Engpässe aussehen könnten, u. a. wie man im Alltag ein Auge auf ältere Menschen haben und sie in ihrem eigenen Zuhause unterstützen kann, um eine Unterbringung im Heim zu vermeiden bzw. diese möglichst lange hinauszuzögern. Schreiben Sie einen Blogpost zum Thema. Fassen Sie dabei folgende Aspekte aus dem Zeitungsartikel auf Seite 63 zusammen:

- Funktionsweise von Alterstechnologie
- wirtschaftliche Argumente für den Einsatz von Alterstechnologie
- Vor- und Nachteile von Alterstechnologie

1 DIE AUFGABE ANALYSIEREN

» SB, S162–163

Ursprungstext: *The future of elder care is here – and it's artificial intelligence*

Mediationstext

- Adressat: ______
- Medium/Textsorte: ______
- Zweck: ______
- Sprachebene: ______

2 DEN INHALT ANALYSIEREN

A Read the text and note down the numbers of the paragraphs which deal with these points.

a Gründe für die Entstehung von Alterstechnologie-Unternehmen ______
b technische Mittel zur Datenerfassung ______
c kommerzieller Anreiz ______
d Nachteile von KI-Technologien ______
e Vorteile von KI-Technologien ______
f für die Mediation nicht relevante Informationen ______

B Match the English words and expressions in the text with their German equivalents. There are two more than you need.

abweichen • auslösen • austricksen • Einwilligung • fördern • Verhaltensmuster • verhindern • Verletzung der Privatsphäre • vernichtend • Warnungen

1 activity patterns ______
2 alerts ______
3 to deviate ______
4 consent ______
5 privacy intrusion ______
6 damning ______
7 to trigger ______
8 to game ______

3 VERFASSEN DER MEDIATION

Schreiben Sie nun Ihren Blogpost.

The future of elder care is here – and it's artificial intelligence

[1] Kellye Franklin recalls the devastation when her now 81-year-old father, a loyal air force veteran, tried to make his own breakfast one morning. Seven boxes of open cereal on the living room floor with milk poured directly into every one of them. He would later be diagnosed with moderate to severe dementia.

[2] Yet Franklin, 39, who is her dad's only child and his primary caregiver, does not worry about that repeating now. In late 2019, she had motion sensors that are connected to an artificial intelligence (AI) system installed in the two-floor townhome she and her dad share in Inglewood, in Los Angeles County. Sensors at the top of doors and in some rooms monitor movements and learn the pair's daily activity patterns, sending warning alerts to Franklin's phone if her dad's normal behavior deviates – for instance if he goes outside and doesn't return quickly. [...]

[3] Welcome to caregiving in the 2020s: in rich societies, computers are guiding decisions about elder care, driven by a shortage of caregivers, an ageing population and families wanting their seniors to stay in their own homes longer. A plethora of so called 'age tech' companies have sprung up over the last few years. [...]

[4] But while there are potential benefits of the technology in terms of safety for older people and a reprieve for caregivers, some also worry about its potential harms. They raise questions around the accuracy of the systems, as well as about privacy, consent and the kind of world we want for our elders. [...]

[5] The system in use in the Franklins' home is called People Power Family. An addition to it, targeted at care agencies, includes daily reports tracking when someone fell asleep, whether they bathed, and bathroom visits. 'You can manage more clients with fewer caregivers' says the promotional video. [...]

[6] For Clara Berridge, who studies the implications of digital technologies used in elder care at the University of Washington, privacy intrusion on older adults is one of the most worrying risks. [...] In 2014, Berridge interviewed 20 non-cognitively-impaired elder residents in a low-income independent living apartment building that used an AI-based monitoring system called QuietCare, based on motion detection. [...]

[7] What she found was damning. The expectation of routine built into the system disrupted the elders' activities and caused them to change their behaviour to try to avoid unnecessary alerts that might bother family members. One woman stopped sleeping in her recliner because she was afraid it would show inactivity and trigger an alert. Others rushed in the bathroom for fear of the consequences if they stayed too long. Some residents begged for the sensors to be removed – though others were so lonely they tried to game the system so they could chat with the operator.

[8] [Franklin] has done her best to explain the monitoring system, for which she now pays $40 a month, simply and without sugar-coating. For the most part, [her father]'s all right with it as long as it helps her.

(506 words)

From: The Guardian, 3 June 20211

Main course

12 The environment

WORKING WITH WORDS

1 VERB + NOUN COLLOCATIONS

>> SB, S162–163

A Match the verbs with nouns from the list as they are used in the text on page 162.

a/the problem • electricity • heat • laws • life • light • the temperature • the world

1 to let in __________
2 to trap __________
3 to support __________
4 to regulate __________
5 to save __________
6 to tackle __________
7 to pass __________
8 to generate __________

B Use some of your answers in A to complete the text. Make any necessary changes.

The earth needs greenhouse gases in its atmosphere because they __________ [1], keeping it at an average of 15 °C. In simple terms, the atmosphere first __________ [2] from the sun. This hits dark surfaces and they become hot. Next, the atmosphere __________ [3] generated by the dark surfaces, i.e. it doesn't let it go back into space. This makes the earth warm and able to __________ [4] in the form of plants, animals and humans. The overproduction of greenhouse gases by humans has produced global warming which could destroy the planet. It is absolutely vital that we __________ [5] of climate change now before it's too late and this means that governments everywhere must act quickly. Above all, they must __________ [6] to make it illegal for people to use fossil fuel vehicles because they are the biggest pollutors.

2 WORD FIELD

>> SB, S166

Complete the mind map with words from the text on page 166 of the SB.

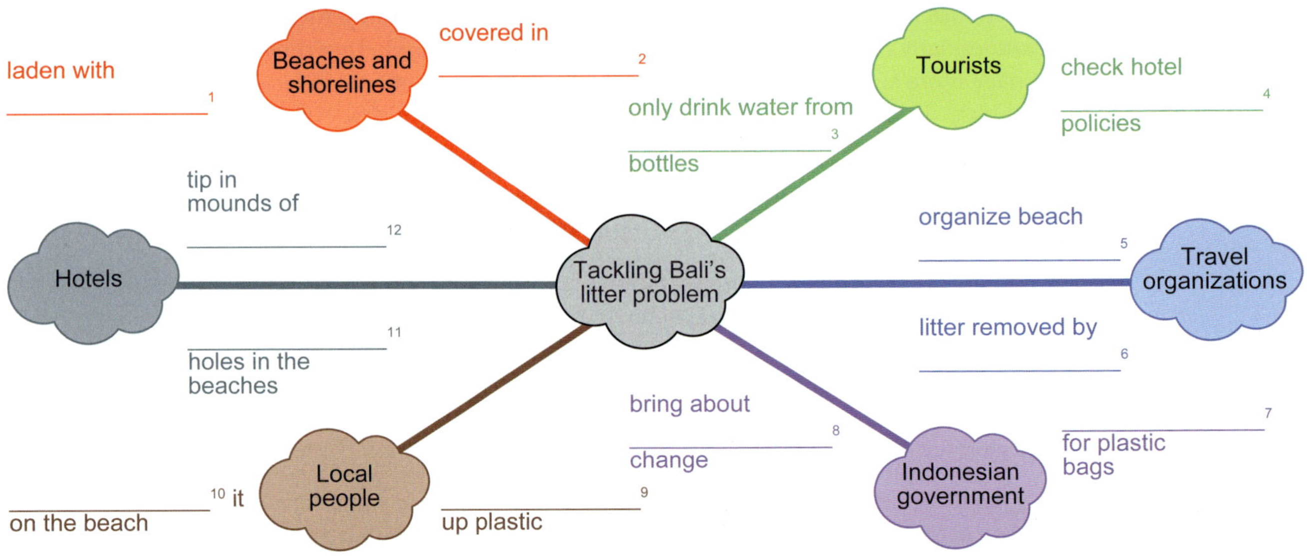

3 WORD FAMILIES

» SB, S170

Complete the gaps with the correct form of the word in brackets. Make any necessary changes.

When in 1998 the Danish island of Samsø decided to take part in a ______________ [1] (compete) to cut greenhouse gas ______________ [2] (to emit) over the next ten years, no one there guessed that it would ______________ [3] (achievement) its goal of energy ______________ [4] (self-sufficient) in half the time. At first, the local ______________ [5] (to reside) were not very ______________ [6] (to enthuse) about the idea and there was considerable ______________ [7] (to resist). However, thanks to the efforts of Søren Hermansen, a local farmer, a ______________ [8] (to solve) was found whereby local people could jointly finance any turbine they could see from their window. This ______________ [9] (to create) answer to a difficult question has made Samsø famous for ______________ [10] (sustainability) energy all over the world.

GRAMMAR

1 IF-SENTENCES TYPE 1

» SB, S163; GF14, S266

Combine the notes below to make at least eight type 1 if-sentences.

Examples:
Global greenhouse gas emissions will fall if we ban fossil fuel cars.
If we don't ban fossil fuel cars, global greenhouse gas emissions won't fall.

1 coastal communities – (not) be at risk
2 global greenhouse gas emissions – (not) fall
3 marine, bird, insect and plant life – (not) suffer
4 the buildings on it – (not) collapse
5 the permafrost – (not) melt
6 the rainforests – (not) become smaller
7 there – be more/less CO_2 in the atmosphere
8 tourists – (not) pollute the mangrove swamps
9 we – (not) protect the coral reefs
10 we – (not) ban fossil fuel cars

2 PARTICIPLE CLAUSES

» SB, S171

Complete the sentences. Use participles and start each answer with before, after, since or while.

How Inuit Nellie Ashevak's house in the Arctic Circle started sinking

1 (she noticed) ______________ ______________ a big crack in the wall of her house, she had never thought about global warming.

2 (she saw) ______________ ______________ the crack, she asked her teacher at school what was happening.

3 He said that (he had started) ______________ ______________ at the school ten years before, he had noticed more and more damage caused by thawing permafrost.

4 Unlike ice, (it thaws) ______________ ______________, it cannot easily refreeze.

5 (it melts) ______________ ______________, it releases carbon dioxide into the atmosphere.

6 (it enters) ______________ ______________ the atmosphere, the carbon speeds up global warming and melts more permafrost

SKILLS: READING

» SB, SF4, S238

1 ANALYSING THE TEXT

A Read the text 'Mass migration on the horizon' on page 67 and tick (✓) the correct definition of 'managed retreat'.

1 a strong and immediate reaction by government agencies and volunteers after a catastrophe ☐
2 moving communities and infrastructure to safer locations in anticipation of extreme weather events ☐
3 using the armed forces to rescue the victims of flooding, hurricanes and earthquakes ☐
4 investing more resources in land reclamation and creation to expand the earth's landmass ☐

B Study the text and note down the paragraphs that refer to these points.

1 climate change ______
2 land creation and reclamation ______
3 managed retreat ______
4 poor people ______
5 rich countries ______
6 wetlands and wildlife habitats ______

C Identify the location(s) mentioned in the text

1 with the worst weather event ______
2 with little chance of survival in the future ______
3 where the poor suffered most ______
4 where the poor will suffer most ______
5 where managed retreat has been successful ______

2 QUESTIONS ON THE TEXT

Use the information in the text to answer the following questions. Write complete sentences using your own words as far as possible.

1 How have humans traditionally expanded the earth's landmass over the centuries?

______
______

2 What made some families unwilling to relocate to higher ground after Hurricane Katrina?

______
______

3 What did thousands of residents in Australia and New Zealand have to do as a result of extreme weather conditions?

______
______

4 Who do the islanders of Kiribati blame for the problems their country is facing?

______
______

5 What will need to be done to the islands of Kiribati if the islanders are to stay there?

______
______

6 How did the UK and California governments widen the floodplains of rivers in coastal areas?

____

____

7 What other beneficial effects did widening the floodplains of rivers have, apart from protecting property?

____

____

8 How is the Indonesian government reacting to the problems facing its capital Jakarta?

____

____

Mass migration on the horizon

[1] Over the centuries man has traditionally fought the elements and pushed back the boundaries of the sea to expand the earth's landmass. The Dutch have their dikes and dams; the iconic Burj Al Arab hotel in Dubai is built on a man-made island; Hong Kong's financial district, airport and Disneyland resort are on land reclaimed from the sea. Now, however, land reclamation and creation are no longer feasible because climate change is raising sea levels with such catastrophic consequences that even the most stubborn climate change deniers cannot ignore them.

[2] In 2005, Hurricane Katrina wreaked havoc on the US city of New Orleans at the mouth of the Mississippi. More than 80% of the area was flooded, at least 1,800 people died and hundreds of thousands were displaced, mainly the poor and elderly in the deprived inner city. Families were offered the chance to relocate to higher ground but this meant the psychological trauma of leaving their homes and communities, never to return.

[3] In July 2022, torrential rain in Sydney, Australia forced over 30,000 people out of their homes when rivers and dams overflowed. A whole year's rainfall fell in just one day and residents are now asking themselves the painful question of whether they will ever be safe in their homes again.

[4] In February 2023, Cyclone Gabrielle devastated New Zealand's North Island with 1,400 people reported missing and 10,500 displaced. It was the worst storm for a century, with 250,000 people left without electricity and many forced to run for their lives to higher ground.

[5] Kiribati in the Pacific is a country of 33 islands two metres or less above sea level and they will all be submerged by 2100. One plan is for the islanders to migrate to Fiji, Australia or New Zealand but they will need government help and retraining to join the workforce there. Another is to dig up sand and rock from the seabed and make the islands higher but for that they will need billions of dollars from the rich countries that caused climate change.

[6] Governments all over the world are getting a loud and clear wake-up call and instead of fighting the elements, or even denying that climate change is happening, some countries (the richer ones in particular) are using a new strategy: managed retreat.

[7] In 2006, 440 hectares of agricultural land along two rivers in the Humber Estuary in the UK were made into the largest floodplain in Europe, thereby protecting 600 properties upstream and creating wetland areas for insects, birds and fish.

[8] Since the megaflood in January 2023, California has been buying up more low-lying residential farming land to widen the floodplains of rivers in vulnerable coastal areas and create new wildlife habitats.

[9] Jakarta, Indonesia's coastal city capital of 10 million people, is sinking into the sea, which is rising due to climate change. The government is planning to move its capital 2,000 km to the island of Borneo but Jakarta's slum-dwellers are expected to be left to their fate. (502 words)

SKILLS: MEDIATION (GERMAN–ENGLISH)

» SB, SF10, S250

1 ANALYSING THE TASK

Read the mediation task below and complete the analysis table.

Situation: Your college is taking part in an international environmental project with partners in Ireland, Finland and Slovenia. A shared website with a blog has been set up to publish participants' contributions. You find the online article on page 69 outlining the major environmental challenges that humanity is facing both now and in the future.

Task: Write a blog post stressing the urgency of the situation. Summarize the following points in the article:
- the three environmental issues described and what is causing them
- the problems that they cause for the world's population
- the measures that must be taken

Analysis of the mediation task

original text: *Drei große Umweltprobleme, die die Zukunft der Menschheit bedrohen*

mediation text
- addressee: ____________________
- medium / text type: ____________________
- purpose: ____________________
- language register: ____________________

2 ANALYSING THE CONTENT

Read the text on page 69 and make notes in English on the following:

environmental issues	what is causing each one
1 ____________________	____________________
____________________	____________________
2 ____________________	____________________
____________________	____________________
3 ____________________	____________________
____________________	____________________

problems the issue causes	measures that could be taken
1 ____________________	____________________
____________________	____________________
2 ____________________	____________________
____________________	____________________
3 ____________________	____________________
____________________	____________________

3 WRITING THE MEDIATION

Write the mediation text in about 100 words.

Drei große Umweltprobleme, die die Zukunft der Menschheit bedrohen

Die Weltgesundheitsorganisation (WHO) schätzt, dass 90 % der Weltbevölkerung verschmutzte Luft einatmet. Einer kürzlich durchgeführten Studie zufolge entspricht das Einatmen der Luft in Neu-Delhi, Indien, an einem Tag dem Rauchen von 125 Zigaretten. Sowohl Indien als auch China mit jeweils über 1,4 Milliarden Einwohnern und andere große Volkswirtschaften weltweit sind bei der Energieversorgung immer noch stark von Kohle und anderen fossilen Brennstoffen abhängig, was zu einer weltweiten Luftverschmutzung und Atemwegserkrankungen führt.

Nach Angaben der WHO haben 2,2 Milliarden Menschen auf der Welt keinen Zugang zu sauberem Trinkwasser. Davon sind 785 Millionen Menschen auf Wasserquellen angewiesen, die mit Fäkalien verunreinigt sind, was sie dem Risiko einer Ansteckung mit durch Wasser übertragenen Krankheiten aussetzt. Darüber hinaus hat schätzungsweise 1 von 3 Menschen weltweit keinen Zugang zu sicheren und angemessenen sanitären Einrichtungen, was zur Verunreinigung von Wasserquellen beitragen kann.

Die Ernährungs- und Landwirtschaftsorganisation der Vereinten Nationen (FAO) hat davor gewarnt, dass der Klimawandel die Lebensmittelsicherheit bedroht. Extreme Wetterereignisse wirken sich auf die Ernteerträge, die Wasserverfügbarkeit und die Viehzucht aus und könnten zu Lebensmittelknappheit und Preissteigerungen führen. Die FAO schätzt, dass weltweit über 800 Millionen Menschen unterernährt sind.

Um die Probleme der Luft- und Wasserverschmutzung und der Ernährungssicherheit zu lösen, sind weltweit radikale Veränderungen erforderlich. Dazu gehören:

- Einstellung der Nutzung fossiler Brennstoffe für praktisch jeden Zweck und Umstellung auf erneuerbare Energien
- ein weltweites Verbot der Verklappung von Industrie- und Chemieabfällen in die Gewässer und massive Investitionen in Wasseraufbereitungsanlagen
- Umstellung von Fleisch- und Milchprodukten auf eine pflanzliche Ernährung, die weniger energieintensiv und resistenter gegen Verunreinigungen ist
- Reduzierung der Lebensmittelverschwendung (1,3 Milliarden Tonnen Lebensmittel werden jedes Jahr verschwendet)
- Anwendung nachhaltiger Verfahren in der Lebensmittelproduktion und Reduzierung des Einsatzes von Pestiziden und Düngemitteln.

(290 words)

SKILLS: TRANSLATION (ENGLISH–GERMAN)

1 WHETHER

Übersetzen Sie folgende Sätze ins Deutsche.

1 Have you asked your father whether he wants to visit us?

2 I often wonder whether the accident was my fault.

3 I can't decide whether to stay or go.

4 I couldn't decide whether to stay or go.

5 They are not sure whether to have children or not.

6 They now have two weeks to decide whether or not to buy the house.

2 MIXED BAG

A Alle vier unten aufgelisteten Verben können verwendet werden, um „reported" im folgenden Satz zu übersetzen. Welches der Verben würden Sie hier verwenden?

berichten • melden • verkünden • angeben

More than half the students who were asked reported feeling overwhelmed by the amount of work they are assigned.

B Übersetzen Sie nun den Satz ins Deutsche und achten Sie dabei besonders auf Folgendes:
– den Einsatz von Artikeln bei „more than half the students"
– eine geschlechtsneutrale Übersetzung von „students"
– die Nebensätze „who were asked" und „they are assigned"
– die Bedeutung von „work" im Englischen im Sinne von „academic work"

3 –ING FORMS

Wörter, die auf *–ing* enden, kommen im Englischen häufig vor. Identifizieren Sie die grammatikalische Form der folgenden Wörter, die auf *–ing* enden, und übersetzen Sie die Sätze ins Deutsche.

1 There are alarm**ing** signs that global warm**ing** is worsen**ing**.

2 She concluded her statement by say**ing** that her feel**ings** were be**ing** hurt by his attitude towards her.

a alarming: ____ d saying: ____

b warming: ____ e feelings: ____

c worsening: ____ f being: ____

Übersetzung:

1 ____

2 ____

4 DIE ÜBERSETZUNG SCHREIBEN

Übersetzen Sie folgenden Text ins Deutsche. Bleiben Sie mit Ihrer Version möglichst nah am Original, aber formulieren Sie trotzdem so, dass es nicht wie eine Übersetzung klingt.

Survey reveals eco-anxiety in young people across the world

A recent survey by Bath University in the UK has revealed alarming degrees of anxiety among young people about climate change. Of the 10,000 interviewees aged 16-25 from all over the world, more than half reported feeling sad, angry, helpless and guilty and 45% stated that their feelings about climate change were having a negative impact on their daily lives. Three quarters felt frightened about the future and betrayed by their governments because politicians were doing too little to combat global warming and its effects on the planet.

Some felt hopeful but more than half believed that humanity was doomed. One young person summed it up by saying that, unlike the older generation, young people feel 'the destruction of the planet is personal'.

Caroline Hickman, the lead author of the survey, explained that it not only measured what young people feel but also what they think and discovered that 40% of respondents were not sure whether to have children or not. One young person said, 'I can't imagine bringing children into a world which is dying.'

The researchers were surprised by the degree of anxiety they encountered and attributed it partly to the fact that children and young people are well aware of the dangers of climate change but virtually powerless to limit its harm and therefore extremely vulnerable to climate anxiety.

(231 words)

SKILLS: WRITING

1 LINKING PHRASES

When writing a text, it is important to use phrases and expressions, such as those in the table below, to structure your ideas so the reader can follow your arguments more easily.

1	**Introducing the topic**	... is/are very much in the news ... is/are an important issue
2	**Introducing an idea**	A case in point is ... A good example is ...
3	**Emphasizing an idea**	It must be pointed out that ... ... is of crucial importance
4	**Listing / Adding ideas**	Firstly, secondly, thirdly, (finally) ... In addition to this, ...
5	**Linking**	both ... and ... not only .... but also
6	**Contrasting**	although + clause despite + noun
7	**Concluding**	All in all, ... Ultimately, ...

Use expressions from the table to turn the following sentences (1–7) into a coherent paragraph. Make any necessary changes. Write the text in your exercise book.

1 Pollution is all over the world.

2 There is a large accumulation of plastic waste in the Pacific Ocean known as the Great Pacific Garbage Patch.

3 The Pacific is not the only place with a plastic waste problem.

4 The United States generates around 37 million tons of plastic waste each year. India generates 9.46 million tons of plastic waste per year. China generates 8.8 million tons of plastic waste per year.

5 Huge amounts of plastic are used in the construction industry. Huge amounts of plastic are used in the packaging industry.

6 Greenpeace has staged dramatic protests, including a 10-metre-long plastic monster called Mr Trash Wheel in the Inner Harbor of Baltimore, Maryland in the United States in 2018. The amount of plastic waste in the world's oceans is expected to triple by 2040.

7 Plastic must be replaced by sustainable materials if the problem is to stop growing year by year.